BEGIN with Jesus

BEGIN *with* Jesus
A 21 Day Devotional

Roberta Whitfield

"To them God has chosen to make known among the Gentiles the glorious riches of this mystery, which is Christ in you, the hope of glory."
-*Colossians 1:27 (Berean Study Bible)*

Xulon Press

Xulon Press
2301 Lucien Way #415
Maitland, FL 32751
407.339.4217
www.xulonpress.com

© 2022 by Roberta Whitfield

All rights reserved solely by the author. The author guarantees all contents are original and do not infringe upon the legal rights of any other person or work. No part of this book may be reproduced in any form without the permission of the author.

Due to the changing nature of the Internet, if there are any web addresses, links, or URLs included in this manuscript, these may have been altered and may no longer be accessible. The views and opinions shared in this book belong solely to the author and do not necessarily reflect those of the publisher. The publisher therefore disclaims responsibility for the views or opinions expressed within the work.

Unless otherwise indicated, Scripture quotations taken from the King James Version (KJV) – public domain, Holy Bible, New International Version (NIV). Copyright © 1973, 1978, 1984, 2011 by Biblica, Inc.™. Used by permission. All rights reserved,Holy Bible, New Living Translation (NLT). Copyright ©1996, 2004, 2007 by Tyndale House Foundation. Used by permission of Tyndale House Publishers, Inc.

Paperback ISBN-13: 978-1-66285-249-7
Hard Cover ISBN-13: 978-1-66285-677-8
Ebook ISBN-13: 978-1-66285-250-3

Dedicated To My Loving Mother Mozella & Sister Parita

Thanks to those that encouraged me along the way:

URFPM; Minister M.; Prayer Warriors; Officer R. Clark; Mrs. C. Eno; Mr. & Mrs. E. Harris; Mrs. M. Jackson; Evangelist C. Jones; Mrs. S. Lyn; Mrs. L. McMillan; Pastors B & J Murray; Mrs. T.Y. Ponds; Minister P. Potts; Pastor M. Staley

And an endless host of family and friends.

Preface

Beloved because of your faith,
May you find favor with
God and please Him---

"And without faith it is impossible to please God, because anyone who approaches Him must believe that He exists and that He rewards those who earnestly seek Him."

---Hebrews 11:6

Beloved, herein is an invitation to you to know that --- God who created the Heavens and the Earth wants to know you, intimately, personally, completely as your Heavenly Father. God is a most perfect Gentleman, He loves us so very much that He allows and gives us the ability to make our own choice, whether we choose to commit, and dedicate our lives to Him and be kept and live, or chose our own way. God will not push Himself upon anyone who will not welcome and receive Him into their hearts and Believe in Him.

> "By The Precious Blood of Jesus Christ with the **authority God has invested in me according to Luke 10:19, "…to trample on snakes and scorpions and to overcome all the power of the enemy**;"

I arrest and bind any and every spirit operating behind anybody, anywhere that may be preventing you from accepting Jesus Christ as Your Lord and personal Savior. I lose love that your heart will be made flesh and turned ever so tenderly toward God. I pray that you will be willing to receive Him as your Lord and personal Savior. Any and every reservation that you may have within you from completely welcoming Jesus Christ into your heart, as Your Lord and personal Savior is undone, rendered null and void.
Tomorrow is not promised to any of us.

The prayers outlined are to be used as a format, but I would also like you to add to the prayers based upon your spiritual needs.

When you are in a desperate situation. Your prayer should be accompanied with and by fasting. Fasting strengthens your faith by drawing you closer to God, when your faith is increased your prayer life releases the strongholds binding the breakthrough in your life. A great example of what prayer and fasting can do in Matthew 17---

After the disciples why they were not able to expel the demonic spirit (lunatic spirit) out of the boy---

And Jesus said unto them, Because of your unbelief: for verily I say unto you, If ye have faith as a grain of mustard seed, ye shall say unto this mountain, Remove hence to yonder place; and it shall remove; and nothing shall be impossible unto you.

Howbeit this kind goeth not out but by ***prayer and fasting.***

----Matthew 17:20-21

Over the past decade as we have moved into the millennium many people have veered away from fasting as a common practice accompanying prayer. As a youngster and new believer growing up, fasting was a regular practice in seeking God within the church. After accepting Jesus Christ as my Lord and personal Savior the elders, ministers and missionaries vehemently concerned with our deliverance and soul salvation moved us onto the next phase. Although the Holy Spirit was hovering over us as new believers or converts through our confession of faith, we did not have the Baptism of the Holy Spirit as evidenced by speaking in tongues. Therefore, we went on a fast asking God to give us the Holy Spirit then later that week attending a corporate church meeting where we tarried for the Baptism of the Holy Spirit and speaking in tongues. After consecrating ourselves throughout the week through prayer and fasting, when joined the corporate church the elders, saints and missionaries who already had the Holy Spirit, proceeded to lay their hands upon us. After that anointing service, all I remember was saying "Hallelujah!" repeatedly, before I was slain in the spirit and spoke in tongues. Let me just say, that I believe every believer can receive the Holy Spirit as in speaking in tongues; it is a walk of faith. Whoever comes to God must first believe that He is, and believe that He is a rewarder of those that diligently seek Him. Receiving the Holy Spirit as in speaking in tongues is part of that reward for diligently seeking God.

I know you have heard it repeatedly that we are living in the last days ----we are! I do believe that there will be an even more outpouring of the Holy Spirit in these last and evil days, because of the multiplication of wickedness, the love of most will grow cold. Do you not see it? Distressing news catapults our ears at the beckoning of each new morning, but know as long as the earth endures, seedtime and harvest, cold and heat, summer and winter, day and night will never cease.

In times like these, you need the Holy Spirit. So the question is --- "Have you received the Holy Spirit since you first believed?" Then you should know that beyond a shadow of a doubt. So how do you know that you have the

Preface

Holy Spirit? You cannot see the Holy Spirit, but you can bear witness of it's effects, it is just like "The wind blows wherever it pleases. You hear its sound, but you cannot tell where it comes from or where it is going. So it is with everyone bon of the spirit." (NIV) (John 3:8) On the Day of Pentecost, they received the Holy Spirit in the upper room. Acts 2 depicts that experience, Acts 2:1-4,

"And when the day of Pentecost was fully come, they were all with one accord in one place. And suddenly there came a sound from heaven as of a rushing mighty wind, and it filled all the house where they were sitting. And there appeared unto them cloven tongues like as of fire, and it sat upon each of them. And they were all filled with the Holy Ghost, and began to speak with other tongues, as the Spirit gave them utterance." (Acts 2:1-4)

There are many different beliefs regarding receiving the Holy Spirit. Some believe that new converts **are automatically through their confession of faith** endowed with the Holy Spirit some believe it's after consecration, prayer and fasting. While others may believe that it is not given as a gift to everyone. We can agree to disagree here but in order for you to have a comforter accompanied with the Spirit that brings you into all truth you need the Holy Spirit. What does it hurt to receive the infilling of the Holy Spirit as referenced by speaking in tongues as they did on the Day of Pentecost. For whoever comes to God must believe that He is, and that He is the rewarder of those that diligently seek Him. Herein is our reward, your diligent seek to know God and the deep things which pertain to God. The Holy Spirit will be there to comfort you, lead and guide you into all truth.

In my personal pursuit of God, I desperately needed the infilling of the Holy Spirit to comfort me and bring me into all truth. It is impossible to make it in this world without assuredly knowing that you are saved, sanctified, and filled with the Holy Spirit. The Holy Spirit is also referenced as the "Holy Ghost," or having been filled through the "Baptism of the Holy Spirit." It is also termed in it's expression as with receiving "Tongues of Fire," tongues are not just speaking to sound like everyone else or sounding like those your ear has heard speaking in tongues. It is an individual personal experience followed as a result of the laying on by the hands of the presbytery, or the elders of your church fold (ex. Acts 8:17). In the church of my youth, we went on a fast first, then tarried for the infilling and baptism of the Holy Spirit. I am not part of the microwave generation but have always preferred everything even my relationship with God to take time. It takes time to live Holy, it takes time for you to be able to let go of who you used to be. I believe that if you ask God for the Holy Spirit, He will give you just that, but it is according to your faith that it will be for you. Be encouraged that if you have not received the infilling of the Holy

Spirit as evidenced by speaking in tongues, it is never too late, but it is an essential part of your spiritual growth but ultimately according to your faith it is given to you. Remember, when you speak in tongues, you do not have to sound like anyone else, you must completely trust and believe in God. Diligently seek God with your whole heart, mind, body and spirit. For lack of a description, speaking in your heavenly language as the Holy Spirit gives you the utterance is like an unexplainable rush of unquenchable fire shut up in your bones when you speak that you cannot contain nor describe. Prophet Jeremiah describes it the best, ----"But if I say, "I will not mention His word or speak anymore in His name," His word is in my heart like a fire, a fire shut up in my bones. I am weary of holding it in; indeed, I cannot." (Jeremiah 20:9) Although Jeremiah is describing in this passage, speaking the words God laid upon his heart, this is a perfect example of the experience of first speaking in tongues as the Spirit of The Living God gives you utterance. Oftentimes, folk may be over-thinking the process of speaking in tongues, it is a gift from God. God is not a respecter of persons, if He gave the gifts of speaking in tongues to one believer, then He will give it to all. God would not withhold withhold any good thing from you. Speaking in tongues is your divine heavenly language that you speak before God privately for your personal edification or corporately for the edification of the Body of Christ. Be encouraged, God is still perfecting those things that concern each and every one of us, our relationship is a process of our faith.

Introduction

In order to fulfill our charge or purpose for why we have been put on earth in such a time as this, we must humbly admit that we need God, without God we are nothing, we cannot even stand in His present in our state of flesh, we need to fully accept Jesus Christ as our personal Lord and Savior as His forgiven,

Some believe there are many roads that lead to God, but that viewpoint is not supported by the biblical scripture in The Holy Bible. However, it does say that "…no man can come through the Father (God) except through Jesus Christ.":

> "Lord," said Thomas, "we do not know where You are going, so how can we know the way?"
>
> **Jesus answered, "I am the way and the truth and the life.**
> **No one comes to the Father except through Me."**
> **If you had known Me, you would know My**

> **Father as well.
> From now on you do know Him and have seen Him."**
> --John 14:6-7

The Bible says,

> **"In Him we have redemption through His blood, the forgiveness of sins, according to the riches of His grace"**
> -Ephesians 1:7

Our debt of sin is fully paid through the redemptive Blood of Jesus Christ,

> **"So Christ was offered once to bear the sins of many.
> To those who eagerly wait for Him He will appear a second time,
> apart from sin, for salvation."**
> --Hebrews 9:28

We are spared from God's wrath, we are made worthy of redemption through Jesus Christ,

Introduction

> **"Much more then, having now been justified by His blood, we shall be saved from wrath through Him. "**
> --Romans 5:9)

We are made alive spiritually through Jesus Christ,

> **"Then Jesus said to them, "Most assuredly, I say to you, unless you eat the flesh of the Son of Man and drink His blood, you have no life in you."**
> --John 6:53)

For there is life in the Blood,

> **"For the life of a creature is in the blood, and I have given it to you to make atonement for yourselves on the altar; it is the blood that makes atonement for one's life."**
> -Leviticus 17:11

We come into this world through the matrix of our mother's womb says, Psalm 51:5, "Behold, I was shaped in iniquity; and in sin did my mother conceive me."

> **"All of us also lived among them at one time, fulfilling the cravings of our flesh and indulging its desires and thoughts. Like the rest, we were by nature children of wrath."**
> ---Ephesians 2:3

We all need salvation, because the truth be told, we are all sinners saved by grace, some of us were blessed enough to know that we are forgiven, that accepted Jesus Christ as our Lord and personal Savior and then there are those who have yet to know Him, those that do not know that they too, are also forgiven----

> **"As it is written, there is none righteous, no not one. There is none that understandeth, there is none that seeketh after God. They are all gone out of the way, they are together become unprofitable; there is none that doeth good, no not one."**
> --Romans 3:10-12

None of us are righteous. As a result of our sinful nature, there is a price, or a consequence for sin. Although, we may enjoy our sinful nature, if that is all we know to do. Fulfilling the lust of our flesh may not be anything that we think of on a regular basis. We just exist in what is familiar or common to us, but still nobody wants to pay an eternal price for the reckless lives we lead. So many of us do not think about sin, we only think about what pleases us, what is temporarily pleasurable. Our life cycle of sin will continue until we have some sort of shift within us like an epiphany to change the direction of our ways. Many of us, were completely side-tracked and blinded by our own impulsive insatiable lust and nature of sin in the moment. We were unable to stop what we were doing, as though we were caught on a landslide just going along with the process unable to even fathom an end to it. Deep down inside, we were comfortable in our sin, we were happy in our sin. Even though, we have allowed our hearts be blinded by sin, it is still so, but lust the pleasure of sin, only last for a minute---- then it dissipates, we can get tired of it. This was my state when I was shacking up, pregnant, a fornicator, unmarried, not certain what I was doing, but was a consenting adult knowing full well it was not right. I knew something was wrong with my overall life's circumstance that I had made for myself, but just continued in it, as though I was watching myself in a stage production. Knowing that there was a price for my disobedience, but praying somehow, I could redeem myself and get back to God in the nick of time. So, I cried out to God in the midst of my sin, asking Him to change the direction that my life was going in. I did not want to live in sin, I just did not know how to stop the unyielding cycle that had me caught up in a whirlwind. It was a cycle that my flesh had co-signed to that my desires held me to. Sin is insatiable, it's never satisfied----it does not lose its grip until we make a conscious decision to turn to God and turn away and repent of our sin, which so easily can beset us,

> **"For the wages of sin is death;
> but the gift of God is eternal life through
> Jesus Christ our Lord."**
> --Romans 6:23

Jesus Christ paid the ultimate price for our wrongdoings, by laying down His life for us. Jesus Christ gave His life because He loved us and believed that we were worth the sacrifice of His precious blood on Calvary's cross. We know that most people would not be willing to die for an upright person, though likely would someone might perhaps be willing to die for a person who is especially good, but Jesus Christ gave His righteous life up, for all of unrighteous mankind. Jesus Christ "who committed no sin, nor was any deceit found in His mouth," (1 Peter 2:22) dies in our place for our sins,

> **"But God commendeth His love toward us,
> in that, while we were yet sinners, Christ
> died for us."**
> --Romans 5:8

I always ask myself, why did Jesus Christ lay down His life for such a wretched soul as me or anyone who has sold themselves to sin? Because Jesus loves us, and wants to restore the broken personal relationship between us and God which existed between mankind since Adam.

"For God so loved the world that He gave His only begotten Son, Jesus Christ, that whosoever believeth in Him should not perish, but have everlasting life."
---John 3;16

We receive salvation and eternal life through our faith in Jesus Christ, and----

"That if thou shalt confess with thy mouth the Lord Jesus, and shalt believe in thine heart that God hath raised Him from the dead, thou shalt be saved. For with the heart man believeth unto righteousness; and with the mouth confession is made unto salvation."
--Romans 10:9-10

"For whosoever shall call upon the Name of The Lord shall be saved."
--Romans 10:13

We are able, **anyone is able** to receive salvation through Jesus Christ, who brings us into a relationship of peace with God:

> "Therefore being justified by faith,
> we have peace with God through our Lord
> Jesus Christ:"
> ---Romans 5:1

> "There is therefore now no condemnation to
> them which are in Christ Jesus,
> who walk not after the flesh, but after
> the Spirit."
> ---Romans 8:1

> "Nay, in all these things we are more than conquerors through Him that loved us. For I am persuaded, that neither death, nor life, nor angels, nor principalities, nor powers, nor things present, nor things to come, Nor height, nor depth, nor any other creature, shall be able to separate us from the
> love of God,
> which is in Christ Jesus our Lord."
> ---Romans 8:37-39

If you have taken the time to read over this section, taking this familiar trip down Roman's Road... won't you join me in making this Confession of Faith?

Introduction

"Heavenly Father,
In the Mighty Name of Jesus Christ,
I come before You -- In Spirit and in Truth,
Asking You to forgive me of every sin that I have ever committed
by thought, by word or by deed against Your Divine Majesty.
I humbly confess with my mouth and believe sincerely in my heart,
That Jesus Christ is Lord.
I believe that Jesus Christ gave His life especially for me on Calvary's Cross
And that He rose on the Third Day from the dead
And now sits on the Right-Hand of God.
I ask You Heavenly Father to come into my heart like never before, totally transform my life – Please Help me!
Change my heart Lord,
so that I will never be the same again.
Heavenly Father, Take out every desire in me that is not like You,
Heavenly Father, Take out any and everything that You have not planted in me according to Matthew 15:13.
I choose from this day forward,
to turn away from all of my sins,
Teach me how to develop a personal

relationship with You on a daily basis.
I want to be one of Your disciples,
I want to be used by You and fulfill my
purpose in You in this earth.
Heavenly Father, I want You to be
pleased with me.
I want to be ready when Your Son, Jesus Christ
returns for Your believers!
For Your word says, that if I confess with my
mouth and believe in my heart that Jesus Christ
is Lord, I am saved.
I have confessed with my mouth
Heavenly Father
And I believe in my heart, that I am Saved.
I am Saved, In Jesus Name. Amen!"

Day 1

"I am the Alpha and the Omega," says the
Lord God,
"who is and who was and who is to come, the
Almighty."

--Revelation 1:8

God is Alpha and Omega, God is the "Beginning of all things" and the "End of all things," that exist, both that which is visible and even that which is invisible--- God is Omniscient meaning that He knows all things; God is Omnipotent, AlMighty God! And has unlimited, able to do anything and everything. God is the very epitome of All Power itself. God is Omnipresent, He is present everywhere and anywhere consecutively, simultaneously - all at the same time without interruption because God is Time. It should be no surprise to you that God knew you when you were yet in your mother's womb **knows every hair on your head**

or the lack thereof. God's inspection of you may even have quickened your embryotic state.

> "O Lord, You have searched me and known *me.*
> You know my sitting down and my rising up;
> You understand my thought afar off.
> You comprehend my path and my lying down,
> And are acquainted with all my ways.
> For *there is* not a word on my tongue,
> *But* behold, O Lord, You know it altogether.
> You have hedged me behind and before,
> And laid Your hand upon me.
> *Such* knowledge *is* too wonderful for me;
> It is high, I cannot *attain* it.
> Where can I go from Your Spirit?
> Or where can I flee from Your presence?
> If I ascend into heaven, You *are* there;
> If I make my bed in hell, behold, You *are there.*
> *If* I take the wings of the morning,
> *And* dwell in the uttermost parts of the sea,
> Even there Your hand shall lead me,
> And Your right hand shall hold me.
> If I say, "Surely the darkness shall fall on me,"
> Even the night shall be light about me;
> Indeed, the darkness shall not hide from You,
> But the night shines as the day;
> The darkness and the light *are* both alike *to You.*
> For You formed my inward parts;

Day 1

You covered me in my mother's womb.
I will praise You, for I am fearfully *and* wonderfully made;
Marvelous are Your works,
And *that* my soul knows very well.
My frame was not hidden from You,
When I was made in secret,
And skillfully wrought in the lowest parts of the earth.
Your eyes saw my substance, being yet unformed.
And in Your book they all were written,
The days fashioned for me,
When *as yet there were* none of them.
How precious also are Your thoughts to me, O God!
How great is the sum of them!
If I should count them, they would be more in number than the sand;
When I awake, I am still with You." (Psalm 139:1-18 NKJV)

Beloveds meditate on Psalm 139 for a moment. This scripture always puts me in a state of awe to imagine that our magnanimous God who created all things, both heaven and earth the Only True and Living God desires to know you and me. As the angels said in Psalm 8:4-6, "What is man, that Thou Art mindful of him? And the son of man, that Thou visitest him? For Thou hast made him a little lower than the angels, and hast crowned him with glory and honour. Thou modest him to have dominion over the works of Thy hands; Thou hast put all things under his feet." I believe that since God is omniscient, He has invested a wealth of purpose in you to reach this world, in such a time as this. In order to fulfill His Great Commision (Matthew 28:16-20).

As you reflect through this 21 Day Devotional, welcome God into your heart. As you come to know Jesus and welcome Him into your heart, you will encounter many different people with different faiths, but because you have a relationship with Jesus you will want them to know Him as you do. I remember ages ago working with a young man, he was of a different faith and asked me about my religious beliefs. I told Him that I was not religious but had a personal relationship with Jesus Christ. He told me that his religion had been in existence over 2000 years. He told me his religion predated Christianity and asked me if I knew that. I did not know how to answer this young man, but in the Bible, it says we should: "Let your speech always be with grace, as though seasoned with salt, **so that you will know how you should respond to each person**." (Colossians 4:6) "but sanctify Christ as Lord in your hearts, **always being ready to make a defense to everyone who asks you to give an account for the hope that is in you**, yet with gentleness and reverence;"(1 Peter 3:15)

I did not want to get into a debate with him. Afterall, God's word is capable of defending itself. God wants people to know Him, more than we do, so I must trust God to give any person with a question the answer they need if I have studied the Bible to show myself approved to Him and not to man. So, as I spoke to him, in my spirit I asked God to give me the words to say. I said, " I am not just a Christian, or a follower of Christ who was born over 2000 years ago, but I am a Judeo-Christian, meaning that my personal relationship with Jesus Christ goes back to, "In the Beginning," of creation. The young man was stunned, he ran out of my cubicle and he never asked me another question again. The best answer we can give anyone is the word of God.

PRAYER

Heavenly Father, I come boldly before the Throne of Grace, knowing that You are faithful and just to forgive me of my sin and cleanse me from all unrighteousness. I ask You to forgive me of any sin that I may have committed by thought, word, or deed against Your divine Majesty. Have Mercy upon me, Have mercy upon me, Most Merciful Heavenly Father. Have mercy upon me, Oh Lord, according to Your lovingkindness. According to the multitude of Your tender mercies, blot out all of my transgressions. Wash me thoroughly from any and all of my iniquities, and cleanse me from my sin. I acknowledge all of my transgressions before You, because You know everything there is to know about me. Forgive me of any secret sin. Forgive me Lord.

I know You desire that I am truthful in every aspect of my life. In my hidden crevices of my heart, You will help me to know wisdom. Purge me, wash me make me clean. I enter into Your gates with Thanksgiving, I enter into Your courts with Praise and I Glorify and Reverence Your Holy Name!

Heavenly Father, You Are my Master, Maker, Creator of all things, Sovereign Lord, King of Kings and Lord of Lords, You Are Alpha and Omega, Majesty! Restore Renew me, fill me up with Your precious Holy Spirit. Let the same mind that is in Christ Jesus, live in me. I bring every thought under the subjection and obedience of Jesus Christ. By the mercies of God, Let me not be conformed by this world: but be transformed by the renewing of my mind, that I will prove what is that good, and acceptable, and perfect, will of God.

1. Lord, You know my beginning and You know my end.

2. Lord, You have searched me and You know me.

3. Lord, You knew me when I was covered in my mother's womb.

4. Lord, You know every hair that is on my head.

5. Lord, You know my sitting down and my rising up.

Day 1

6. Lord, You know the very thoughts and intents of my heart.

7. There is nothing hidden from You!

8. For You Heavenly Father are acquainted with all my ways.

9. For there is not a word on my tongue, that You do not know.

10. Lord, You laid Your hand upon me, You have sent Your angels to encamp round about me and protect me in all my ways.

11. There is no place that I can go from Your Spirit, There is no where to flee from Your Presence. 12. Even though by my wicked deeds, I made my bed up in hell.

13. Even in the darkest places You are there.

14. Lord You will never forsake me,

15. Lord, You promised that if I harken diligently unto Your voice

16. Lord if I obey Your commandments

17. Lord teach me Your ways that You will be pleased with me.

18. Lord let my will line up with Your will for my life

19. Lord, I don't want to lean to my understanding, guide and lead me.

20. Lord, make all of my crooked paths straight.

21. Lord, let me trust in You, because You will direct my paths.

22. Lord You are light, even in my darkest hour.

23. Lord, let Your light shine in me that men will see Your good works in me and glorify You!

24. Cover and protect me, shield me, shield me above, shield me below.

25. Lord be a shield all around me.

I am chosen, a royal priesthood, a holy nation, I am God's own possession set apart for Your Holy purpose. I am peculiar, proclaiming the virtues of God who has called me out of darkness and brought me into this marvelous light.

Day 1

By the authority that God has invested in me since the foundation of time, I soak and saturate my prayers in the precious Blood of Jesus Christ. I decree and declare divine immunity according to Psalm 91: "I dwell in the secret place of the most High and abide under the shadow of the Almighty. Lord You are my refuge and my fortress: my God; in You I will trust."

I know that every good and perfect gift that comes down from the Father of lights is already mine in Jesus Name. Let the meditation of my heart and the words of my mouth be acceptable in Your sight, Oh Lord my God, Nothing and No one compares to You. You are my strength, You are all of my sustenance, You The Only True and Living God, You Are my Redeemer. In Jesus Name. Amen!

Day 2

> "Behold, how good and how pleasant it is
> For brethren to dwell together in unity!
> It is like the precious oil upon the head,
> Running down on the beard,
> The beard of Aaron,
> Running down on the edge of his garments.
> It is like the dew of Hermon,
> Descending upon the mountains of Zion;
> For there the Lord commanded the blessing ---
> Life forevermore."--Psalm 133 NKJV

This is Day Two of your devotional reading, as we survey the number 2 from a biblical context, means "union." Union is the joining of two. Whether it is the union of a man and a woman, made one in marriage or the union of Jesus Christ with the church. Everything in union works cohesively with comradery, without division. In this age there are many divisions even amongst different churches and those within the churches or Houses of Prayer. We may have different giftings within that body that house, but we all have a purpose. "That there should be no schism in the body; but that the members should have the same care one for another. And whether one member suffer, all the members suffer with it; or one member be honoured, all the members rejoice with it. Now ye are the body of Christ, and members in particular." (1 Corinthians 12:25-27)

There is no competition in Christ, we must all delight in working toward one common goal, which is to spread the Gospel of Jesus Christ, as Ambassadors of the Great Commission. "We have different gifts, according to the grace given to each of us. If your gift is prophesying, then prophesy in accordance with your faith; if it is serving, then serve; if it is teaching, then teach; if it is to encourage, then give encouragement; if it is giving then give generously; if it is to lead, do it diligently; if it is to show mercy, do it cheerfully." (Romans 12:6-8 NIV) For "The eye cannot say to the hand, "I don't need you!" And the head cannot say to the fee, "I don't need you!" (1 Corinthians 12:21 NIV) The Bible reminds us to, "Be devoted to one another with [authentic] brotherly affection [as members of one family], give preference to one another in honor;" (Romans 12:10 AMP) If we are busy bickering, competing, acting as though we are superior... then how can we combat our real enemy which is not one another and have victory over the enemy? We must continually pray for our Houses of Prayer, the Pastors and leadership.

Day 2

Ask God to give you someone in your church setting, local community, or place of employment to pray for, that you meet on a regular basis without letting anyone know. Pray for their entire wholeness in every aspect of their lives, as The Lord instructs you. Pray for their family, marriages, children, relatives, career endeavors and every aspect of their lives. This may be for a short timespan or **may** take several years. Let God direct your path.

PRAYER

Heavenly Father, I come boldly before the Throne of Grace, knowing that You are faithful and just to forgive me of my sin and cleanse me from all unrighteousness. I ask You to forgive me of any sin that I may have committed by thought, word, or deed against Your divine Majesty. Have Mercy upon me, Have mercy upon me, Most Merciful Heavenly Father. Have mercy upon me, Oh Lord, according to Your lovingkindness. According to the multitude of Your tender mercies, blot out all of my transgressions. Wash me thoroughly from any and all of my iniquities, and cleanse me from my sin. I acknowledge all of my transgressions before You, because You know everything there is to know about me. Forgive me of any secret sin. Forgive me Lord. I know You desire that I am truthful in every aspect of my life. In my hidden crevices of my heart, You will help me to know wisdom. Purge me, wash me make me clean. I enter into Your gates with Thanksgiving, I enter into Your courts with Praise and I Glorify and Reverence Your Holy Name!

Heavenly Father, You Are my Master, Maker, Creator of all things, Sovereign Lord, King of Kings and Lord of Lords, You Are Alpha and Omega, Majesty! Restore Renew me, fill me up with Your precious Holy Spirit. Let the same mind that is in Christ Jesus, live in me. I bring every thought under the subjection and obedience of Jesus Christ. By the mercies of God, Let me not be conformed by this world: but be transformed by the renewing of my mind, that I will prove what is that good, and acceptable, and perfect, will of God.

I am chosen, a royal priesthood, a holy nation, I am God's own possession set apart for Your Holy purpose. I am peculiar, proclaiming the virtues of God who has called me out of darkness and brought me into this marvelous light.

1. In Your word Heavenly Father, it says that You command a blessing in unity.

2. Bless our families, church families, Pastor(s) and Leaders.

3. Give our Pastor(s), Chief servants of Your House of Prayer, courage and strength.

Day 2

4. Give our Pastor(s), Chief servants of Your House of Prayer, the will and the ability to carry out Your will.

5. Restore, renew and refresh our Pastor(s), Chief servants and Leaders so that they will not grow weary in well doing.

6. Give our Pastor(s), Chief servants and Leaders of Your House of Prayer an ability to seek You in order to see clearly Your vision for the ministry.

7. Give our Pastor(s), Chief servants and Leaders Your wisdom to have insight and foresight.

8. Strengthen and cover our Pastor(s), Chief servants and Leaders family home life, so that there will be no lack of any kind within their households, in love, in nurturing, so that their spouse(s) and children lives as a result of their commitment to ministry will flourish.

9. Lord, we ask that You bind us together in the unity of sisterly and brotherly love.

10. Teach us how to protect and speak well of our fellow brethren, those in the body of Christ that labor among us. For love covers a multitude of sin.

11. Teach us How to prefer the saints, that we love others earnestly as You Our Heavenly Father have also love us!

12. Teach us how to walk in obedience and be pleasing to You in every aspect of our lives.

13. Teach us how to obey Your voice and keep Your covenants.

14. Let our church family prosper in every aspect of their lives and be in good health even as our souls are already prospering.

15. Let there be no lack financially, emotionally, perfect all those things that concern each and every one of us so that there will be no lack of any kind in their households.

16. Set us aside as Your treasured possessions out of all the people on the face of the earth.

By the authority that God has invested in me since the foundation of time, I soak and saturate my prayers in the precious Blood of Jesus Christ. I decree and declare divine immunity according to Psalm 91: "I dwell in the secret place of the most High and abide under the shadow of the

Almighty. Lord You are my refuge and my fortress: my God; in You I will trust."

I know that every good and perfect gift that comes down from the Father of lights is already mine in Jesus Name. Let the meditation of my heart and the words of my mouth be acceptable in Your sight, Oh Lord my God, Nothing and No one compares to You. You are my strength, You are all of my sustenance, You are The Only True and Living God, You Are my Redeemer. In Jesus Name. Amen!

Day 3

"For in Christ all the fullness of the Diety lives in bodily form, and in Christ you have been brought to fullness. He is the head over every power and authority." --Colossians 2:9-10 NIV

"For in Christ lives all the fullness of God in a human body. So you also are complete through your union with Christ, who is the head over every ruler and authority." --Colossians 2:9-10 NLT

"For in Him dwells all the fullness of the Godhead bodily; And you have been made complete in Christ, who is the head over every ruler and authority." --Colossians 2:9-10 KJV

One of the most profound lessons I had to realize is that the Holy Spirit is already complete in us! The Holy Spirit doesn't need any modifications, nothing needs to be added to it and nothing needs to be taken away. Before we were made manifest into this world, we had a pre-mortal existence, we were perfect and existed as spirit beings and lived in a spirit world in the presence of our Heavenly Father. Then through our birth process through the matrix of our mother's womb, we became human beings with flesh and were exposed to this world. We are a spirit that lives within flesh. We were shaped in iniquity, and in sin did our mother's conceive us. Anything that our Heavenly Father did not plant, let it be routed out. God is the Great Physician and there is nothing or no one that is beyond or incapable of being healed by Him. No one is ever too broken for God. God will purposefully use the most broken people to do some of the most amazing and miraculous things that can confound those who believed they were wise. God already knew about the things that seem as though they are flaws in us. We are a peculiar people, set apart for God's Holy purpose. God never makes any mistakes. God will never leave us ashamed. God doesn't have to ask anyone's permission or consult anyone about His decisions. God chose you before the foundation of this earth. God can use everyone despite any of our short comings for His Glory. God can turn around any situation, that even what the enemy meant for evil, God can turn it around for our good. I believe God shows off His masterful capabilities in some of the most extraordinary miraculous ways in the most seemingly imperfect underestimated vessels. God magnifies His immutable undeniable miracle working power in that obscure unlikely person. So that the Glory may be seen of God and not in us, the individual. So that no one will be able to glory in His presence.

PRAYER

Heavenly Father, I come boldly before the Throne of Grace, knowing that You are faithful and just to forgive me of my sin and cleanse me from all unrighteousness. I ask You to forgive me of any sin that I may have committed by thought, word, or deed against Your divine Majesty. Have Mercy upon me, Have mercy upon me, Most Merciful Heavenly Father. Have mercy upon me, Oh Lord, according to Your loving kindness. According to the multitude of Your tender mercies, blot out all of my transgressions. Wash me thoroughly from any and all of my iniquities, and cleanse me from my sin. I acknowledge all of my transgressions before You, because You know everything there is to know about me. Forgive me of any secret sin. Forgive me Lord. I know You desire that I am truthful in every aspect of my life. In my hidden crevices of my heart, You will help me to know wisdom. Purge me, wash me make me clean. I enter into Your gates with Thanksgiving, I enter into Your courts with Praise and I Glorify and Reverence Your Holy Name!

Heavenly Father, You Are my Master, Maker, Creator of all things, Sovereign Lord, King of Kings and Lord of Lords,

You Are Alpha and Omega, Majesty! Restore Renew me, fill me up with Your precious Holy Spirit. Let the same mind that is in Christ Jesus, live in me. I bring every thought under the subjection and obedience of Jesus Christ. By the mercies of God, Let me not be conformed by this world: but be transformed by the renewing of my mind, that I will prove what is that good, and acceptable, and perfect, will of God.

1. Lord, we thank You that "For His fullness [Jesus Christ] we have all received grace upon grace." (John 1:16)

2. Lord, we thank You "That God was reconciling the world to Himself in Christ, not counting men's trespasses against them. And He has committed to us the message of reconciliation." (2 Corinthians 5:19)

3. Lord, according to Jeremiah 1:5 we know that "Before I formed you in the womb I knew you; Before you were born I sanctified you; I ordained you a prophet to the nations."

I am chosen, a royal priesthood, a holy nation, I am God's own possession set apart for Your Holy purpose. I am peculiar, proclaiming the virtues of God who has called me out of darkness and brought me into this marvelous light.

Day 3

By the authority that God has invested in me since the foundation of time, I soak and saturate my prayers in the precious Blood of Jesus Christ. I decree and declare divine immunity according to Psalm 91: "I dwell in the secret place of the most High and abide under the shadow of the Almighty. Lord You are my refuge and my fortress: my God; in You I will trust."

I know that every good and perfect gift that comes down from the Father of lights is already mine in Jesus Name. Let the meditation of my heart and the words of my mouth be acceptable in Your sight, Oh Lord my God, Nothing and No one compares to You. You are my strength, You are all of my sustenance, You The Only True and Living God, You Are my Redeemer. In Jesus Name. Amen!

Day 4

"But seek first his kingdom and his righteousness, and all these things will be given to you as well." ---Matthew 6:33

During this pandemic, it is no longer about religion, but about our personal relationship with Jesus Christ. We should have learned to put into practice privately what we have been taught in church. In these last days, we must develop our own personal relationship with Jesus Christ. We have to learn to get so close to God by letting His word abide in us and purify us. We have to cry out to God and know Him for ourselves and know that He is hearing and answering our prayers.

Like many of you, I didn't grow up in a silver spoon in my mouth, but somehow in my modest household was a home filled with an abundance of love, joy, peace and laughter. When I think about my childhood it always brings joy to my heart as I look forward to the future that God has laid out for me. Like so many others, we made the best of what we had and were grateful. I was thankful for every single blessing that God gave bestowed upon me. We took nothing for granted. My mother and father were known as loving, kind, humble and considerate within our small community. My mother was the first person that introduced me to God and taught me to reverence Him and that He really existed. I remember whenever there was a thunder or lightning storm in our midst, my mother would tell me and my brother to sit quietly on the living room couch and she would swiftly survey our apartment unplugging any electric apparatus that was attached to the main outlets. She would settle down after she was certain everything was secure, then join us in the living room. We were taught never to take God for granted, never to take God's Name in vain. We were taught from the word that those that took God's name in vain did not reverence or love God and were His enemies. The Bible says that God will not hold anyone guiltless that takes His Name in vain. We were also taught that the fear of The Lord, was the beginning of wisdom. So, as we would sit quietly, startled by the loud thunder, my mother would reassure us by calming our fears and tell us that we had to be still as God moved and rearranged His furniture.

As a child, I carried that same sentiment by honoring God in my heart. I did not go to God with an agenda, because I did not know how to have one. I first went to church because my parents told me to and in the process of my obedience I fell hopelessly in love with God. Unbeknownst to me, I was seeking first God's Kingdom and His Righteousness with my whole heart, soul and spirit and not even aware that I was doing it. My obedience and servanthood did not go unnoticed by God. All those that serve the Lord even in the smallest capacity, those who are considered the least among us are the greatest among us in the household of faith. I sought just to know God and let Him order all of my steps. As we abide in God and His word, He will abide in us, as we move closer to God, He is moving closer to us. As we commit our way to God, He is able to keep those who are committed to Him.

PRAYER

Heavenly Father, I come boldly before the Throne of Grace, knowing that You are faithful and just to forgive me of my sin and cleanse me from all unrighteousness. I ask You to forgive me of any sin that I may have committed by thought, word, or deed against Your divine Majesty. Have Mercy upon me, Have mercy upon me, Most Merciful Heavenly Father. Have mercy upon me, Oh Lord, according to Your lovingkindness. According to the multitude of Your tender mercies, blot out all of my transgressions. Wash me thoroughly from any and all of my iniquities, and cleanse me from my sin. I acknowledge all of my transgressions before You, because You know everything there is to know about me. Forgive me of any secret sin. Forgive me Lord.

I know You desire that I am truthful in every aspect of my life. In my hidden crevices of my heart, You will help me to know wisdom. Purge me, wash me make me clean. I enter into Your gates with Thanksgiving, I enter into Your courts with Praise and I Glorify and Reverence Your Holy Name!

Heavenly Father, You Are my Master, Maker, Creator of all things, Sovereign Lord, King of Kings and Lord of Lords, You Are Alpha and Omega, Majesty! Restore Renew me, fill me up with Your precious Holy Spirit. Let the same mind that is in Christ Jesus, live in me. I bring every thought under the subjection and obedience of Jesus Christ. By the mercies of God, Let me not be conformed by this world: but be transformed by the renewing of my mind, that I will prove what is that good, and acceptable, and perfect, will of God.

1. Lord, I lay aside every single weight that so easily beset me.

2. Lord, purify me.

3. Lord, I come before You, seeking only Your perfect will for my life.

4. Lord, let my will and line up and conform to Your will.

5. Lord, I ask that You take away anything in me that You are not pleased with in my life.

6. Lord I ask that You remove anything in me that is not what You have originally planted in me.

I am chosen, a royal priesthood, a holy nation, I am God's own possession set apart for Your Holy purpose. I am peculiar, proclaiming the virtues of God who has called me out of darkness and brought me into this marvelous light.

By the authority that God has invested in me since the foundation of time, I soak and saturate my prayers in the precious Blood of Jesus Christ. I decree and declare divine immunity according to Psalm 91: "I dwell in the secret place of the most High and abide under the shadow of the Almighty. Lord You are my refuge and my fortress: my God; in You I will trust."

I know that every good and perfect gift that comes down from the Father of lights is already mine in Jesus Name. Let the meditation of my heart and the words of my mouth be acceptable in Your sight, Oh Lord my God, Nothing and No one compares to You. You are my strength, You are all of my sustenance, You The Only True and Living God, You Are my Redeemer. In Jesus Name. Amen!

Day 5

> "When He [Jesus] was come down from the mountain, great multitudes followed Him. And, behold, there came a leper and worshipped Him, saying, Lord, if thou wilt, thou canst make me clean. And Jesus put forth His hand, and touched him, saying, I will; be thou clean. And immediately his leprosy was cleansed."
>
> --- Matthew 8:1-3

One of the most frightening diseases during the first century was leprosy. There was no cure, and just the unsightly way this disease ravaged the human body left those who came into proximity with it and those who had it traumatized. Leviticus 5:2-3 mandated that Leprosy and any disease like it, would have marked those who were exposed to it as sinful and unclean. Most townspeople would have caused anyone to avoid those who had it, at all costs. Simply coming into close contact with a person that they thought was exposed caused calamity. They would have deemed those who dared to cross the line who came into close proximity with those with leprosy as unclean and sinful as well. Lepers lived a sequestered and isolated existence. Throughout history and modern culture, there has always been a stigma attached any disease, that is highly contagious, especially those diseases that we have little or no information. Much of their apprehension regarding leprosy in the first century would probably be the same as we would respond to it today. In most cases, we would not know the origin or how the disease was contracted and spread to others. Our first line of defense would have been to avoid the person who had the disease, or those who we thought had it altogether. We would have ignored them and would not have touched them. We would not have shook their hands, hugged them, or sat next to a person with leprosy under any circumstances. The only reference they would have had was that the person with leprosy was sinful and unclean, and they needed to be avoided at all costs. These people would have been deemed outcast from their communities and lived an isolated existence outside of the camp away from their close family members, relatives, and friends unless they would have also risked contamination. Most colonies of leprose people would have migrated together to find a sense of belonging, since they were all set apart from the general population. Leprosy went through a series of stages, where a person's skin would show slow signs of a light pigmentation change, red skin patches or ulcerated blisters which would cause a loss of sensation, nerve damage or numbness over a period. The atrophy would spread and if it was a limb, it could completely weaken, deteriorate, then eventually dry up and fall off. You can imagine the hysteria of those who witnessed these symptoms. Victims of leprosy suffered in silence, not only from the outward appearance, but the emotional damage it must have caused. In addition, the affected body part would have crippled their hands, feet, causing a type of paralysis due to nerve damage and in some cases even blindness. On top of the apparent physical ailment, those infected lived an isolated existence, emotionally rendered as outcast, having to avoid and being avoided by their own communities. Anyone who knew someone had leprosy would detour the place where they lived, as news spread, they would eventually be labeled unclean and eventually forced to leave their immediate communities. Scriptures confirm that Jesus Christ performed several miracles healing even those with leprosy, one desperate man confronted Jesus and begged him on his knees, saying "if you are willing, you can make me clean." Jesus replied by reaching out and touching the man to comfort him and said, "I am willing," and He went on further to say "…be clean." Jesus also asked the man not to tell anyone that he was healed, but the man probably so overwhelmed could not refrain from telling everyone of his miraculous healing. Certainly, every person who had leprosy heard rumors that they could also be healed and those who knew them more than likely spread the news too. As a result, once word got around, Jesus could no longer remain in that town openly. They still found Jesus even in desert places, so that He could heal them. I am certain there were more circumstances and situations when Jesus healed those with leprosy, but there is only one man healed told from the different perspectives of The Book of Matthew (Matthew 8:1-3), The Book of Mark (Mark 1:40-45) and The Book of Luke (Luke 5:12-13). Luke also told of the healing of ten lepers at one time (Luke 17:17). Although, there are only eleven instances documented in scripture, when Jesus heals lepers, we know that there must have been more. John 21:25 confirms this, when it states, "And there are also many other things which Jesus did, the which, if they should be written everyone, I suppose that even the world itself could not contain the books that should be written. Amen."

Jesus' willingness to touch a person labeled "contaminated," "untouchable" and "detestable," without reservation, is a proclamation that He is also willing to do the same for us. He redeems us no matter what our state, both physically and spiritually; sinless and clean, bringing us back into our rightful relationship with God.

Meditate on the unmerited grace and mercy that God shows toward us. God is not a respecter of persons, He does not play favorites. Reflect on how God is always willing and able to redeem us.

Day 5

PRAYER

Heavenly Father, I come boldly before the Throne of Grace, knowing that You are faithful and just to forgive me of my sin and cleanse me from all unrighteousness. I ask You to forgive me of any sin that I may have committed by thought, word, or deed against Your divine Majesty. Have Mercy upon me, Have mercy upon me, Most Merciful Heavenly Father. Have mercy upon me, Oh Lord, according to Your lovingkindness. According to the multitude of Your tender mercies, blot out all of my transgressions. Wash me thoroughly from any and all of my iniquities, and cleanse me from my sin. I acknowledge all of my transgressions before You, because You know everything there is to know about me. Forgive me of any secret sin. Forgive me Lord. I know You desire that I am truthful in every aspect of my life. In my hidden crevices of my heart, You will help me to know wisdom. Purge me, wash me make me clean. I enter into Your gates with Thanksgiving, I enter into Your courts with Praise and I Glorify and Reverence Your Holy Name!

Heavenly Father, You Are my Master, Maker, Creator of all things, Sovereign Lord, King of Kings and Lord of Lords, You Are Alpha and Omega, Majesty! Restore Renew me, fill me up with Your precious Holy Spirit. Let the same mind that is in Christ Jesus, live in me. I bring every thought under the subjection and obedience of Jesus Christ. By the

mercies of God, Let me not be conformed by this world: but be transformed by the renewing of my mind, that I will prove what is that good, and acceptable, and perfect, will of God.

1. Lord, teach me how to repent daily, for this is the daily bread that You give us.

2. Therefore, today, I come boldly before the throne of grace knowing that You are faithful and just to forgive me of all my sin and cleanse me from all unrighteousness.

3. I rededicate my life back to You;

4. Lord, Redeem me back to You!

5. Lord, forgive me of any sin that I have committed against Thy divine righteousness, by thought, word or deed.

6. Lord, Redeem me back to a right relationship with You, both spiritually and physically. According to Matthew 15:13, rout out anything in me that you did not plant in me. "Have mercy upon me, Lord, according to thy lovingkindness: according unto the multitude of Your tender mercies blot out my transgressions. Wash me thoroughly and completely

from mine iniquity, and cleanse me from my sin. For I acknowledge my transgressions: and my sin is ever before me. Against You, have I sinned, and done evil in Your sight: that You will be justified when You speak, and be clear when You judge. Lord, I am aware that I was shaped in iniquity; and in sin did my mother conceive me. Behold, You desire truth in my inward parts: and in the hidden part You will make me to know wisdom. Purge me with hyssop, and I shall be clean: wash me, and I shall be whiter than snow. Make me to hear joy and gladness; that the bones which You have broken may rejoice.

7. Lord, I know that "What comes out of a person is what defiles them. For it is from within, out of a person's heart, that evil thoughts come – sexual immorality, theft, murder, adultery, greed, malice, deceit, lewdness [which is indecency, obscenity; vulgar sexual character or behavior], envy, slander, arrogance, and folly. All these evils come from inside and defile a person." (Scripture reference Mark 7:20-23)

8. Lord, You always see the best in us and desire a personal relationship with us. If we chose to abide in Your word so that You can abide in us.

9. Lord, purify me from everything that contaminates my body, soul (will, emotions and thoughts dwell) and spirit.

10. Lord perfect holiness out of y reference toward You. In Jesus Name.

11. Lord, create in me a pure heart and renew a steadfast spirit within me.

12. Lord, I know if I confess my sins (any of my wrongdoing, things that I am aware of, that you will have mercy on me for those unconscious thoughts and those things that I am not aware of.)

13. Lord, I ask You for mercies sake to rout out anything in me that is not pleasing to You.

14. Lord, Grant me through redemption to walk in Your light, as You are in the light that I may have an unhindered personal relationship with You. That You will have complete fellowship with me.

15. For, I have accepted Jesus Christ as My Lord and personal savior who purifies me from all sin.

16. Lord, please do not hid Your face from my sins, and blot out all mine iniquities.

17. Create in me a clean heart, Lord; and renew a right spirit within me.

18. Lord, please do not cast me away from Your presence;

19. Lord do not take Your presence within me, the indwelling of the holy spirit from me.

20. Lord, please restore in me the joy of Your salvation;

21. Lord, please uphold me with Your spirit.

22. Then I will be Your disciple, able to teach transgressors Your ways; so that those who do not know You will be converted to You and brought into a whole (right) personal relationship with You.

23. Lord, deliver me from blood guiltiness that comes with sin,

24. Lord, You alone are my salvation

25. Let my tong sing aloud of Your righteousness

26. Lord, let my lips speak in Praise of You!
27. Thank You Heavenly Father for redeeming me back to You!

28. Lord, Thank You or redeeming me and giving me the strength turn away from our wicked ways.

I am chosen, a royal priesthood, a holy nation, I am God's own possession set apart for Your Holy purpose. I am peculiar, proclaiming the virtues of God who has called me out of darkness and brought me into this marvelous light.

By the authority that God has invested in me since the foundation of time, I soak and saturate my prayers in the precious Blood of Jesus Christ. I decree and declare divine immunity according to Psalm 91: "I dwell in the secret place of the most High and abide under the shadow of the Almighty. Lord You are my refuge and my fortress: my God; in You I will trust."

I know that every good and perfect gift that comes down from the Father of lights is already mine in Jesus Name. Let the meditation of my heart and the words of my mouth be acceptable in Your sight, Oh Lord my God, Nothing and No one compares to You. You are my strength, You are all of my sustenance, You The Only True and Living God, You Are my Redeemer. In Jesus Name. Amen!

Day 6

"And he said, The things which are impossible with men are possible with God."--Luke 18:27

When we take the word **impossible** and break it down, we can see clearly that impossible can be broken up to state: **"I-M-Possible,"** as if to say with God anything with Him is possible. In fact, Jesus replied, "What is impossible for man is made possible with God." God has designed a special miracle in your life, especially for you. God wants to use you as a vessel as His conduit to make that miracle manifest in this earth realm. God is still not a respecter of persons. God wants to do an Exceedingly, Abundantly, Beyond all that you could ever ask or think, not only in your life, but to show off in your life, just as He has showed off in the lives of the lives of those memorialized in the "Hall of Faith," Noted in the Book of Hebrews, Chapter 11. God begins the chapter saying, "No faith is the substance of things hoped for, the evidence of things not seen." (Hebrews 11:1) Beloved, what are you hoping for, what is your desire, what do you need God to do for you? Whatever that thing is you need to cry out to Him and let it be known. We have to realize exactly what a trial is, (as a noun)---in a court of law "a formal examination of evidence before a judge, and typically before a jury, in order to decide guilt in a case of a criminal or civil proceedings," ----it can also be described as, "a test of the performance, qualities, or suitability of someone or something."

However---(as a verb) "action word," it's a "TEST" something, especially a new product to assess it's suitability or performance." I'd like to add here that it is an endurance test of your faith. Whatever you may be dealing with, that situation and circumstance was not brought to your doorstep by happenstance, No-No-No! I believe that when you are a child of the Utmost High God that it cannot defeat you, but it is an endurance test of your faith. Listen to what Jesus says in Luke 22:29:

> "And I confer on you a kingdom, just as my
> Father conferred one on me, so that you may eat
> and drink at my table in my kingdom and sit
> on thrones,
> judging the twelve tribes of Israel.
> "Simon, Simon, satan has asked to sift **all of you**
> as wheat.
> **But I have prayed for you**, Simon, that your faith
> may not fail.
> And when you have turned back, strengthen your
> brothers." ---Luke 22:29-32

Day 6

Let me just give you a clue, I do not want you to think it strange regarding a fiery trial in your life, even if some really strange unexplainable things happen to you. No matter what it looks like right now, God is going to give you the victory to the point that spectators will not believe what God has done for you. Remember, that when a great door has been opened to you, there will be many adversaries. They are not your enemies per say, but God's enemies. There is a battle going on in the unseen realm of good and evil. And we all know that good always triumphs over evil. Don't you know the plans that God has for you? They are plans that are "good," and not evil, because God wants to give you a future and a hope, not only for you but for your children and your children's children. God want's to make an open spectacle of the enemy that came with everything that it had to thwart your destiny to find itself empty and impotent and that it did not work. For this is your heritage Beloved: "No weapon formed against you shall prosper and every tongue that's turned against you is already condemned!" The adversary, in order to thwart the purpose of God over your life has undoubtedly totally underestimated you, both the enemy and it's cohorts are incapable of discerning "Christ in you," the Hope of Glory! While it was looking to and fro trying to devour God's Beloved, you were handpicked by the enemy, just like Job, because it thought you did not have the wherewithal to overcome. Certainly, it did not see that you were not alone in that fiery trial. Just like it was for Daniel, there was a fourth man in that fiery trial with you. The enemy has underestimated your stamina to hold up under a trial and believe it or not even though you may think you are ready to topple over and faint, "I decree and declare, by the power of God that He has invested in His disciples, before the foundation of time---that you are already victorious!" Aside from what you may believe, God has not put more on you than you can bear. Not only can you bear it, **but you were made for it**, you were made for such a time as this! When we look back at this passage in Luke 22:32, we see the name Simon, well in John 1:42, there is a name change--- "When Jesus looked at him, He said: "You are Simon, the son of John; you will be called Ce'phas" (which is translated 'Peter")." Cephas is a common noun which means stone or rock. Don't you just love it when God sends His angels to speak a prophetic declaration into your life? Well, Jesus was speaking to Peter prophetically and He was calling Peter a rock, a stone.

Beloved when you come out of a fiery trial you will not be the same, everything that came to overthrow you, you will overthrow. God will use you to dominate over the enemy of your life, because you were never alone.

Everything that the enemy meant for evil, everything that the enemy sent to defeat you, God Said that He is turning it all around, For His Glory, For His Honor For His Namesake! Don't forget to tell them that it was Jesus that brought you through!

Day 6

PRAYER

Heavenly Father, I come boldly before the Throne of Grace, knowing that You are faithful and just to forgive me of my sin and cleanse me from all unrighteousness. I ask You to forgive me of any sin that I may have committed by thought, word, or deed against Your divine Majesty. Have Mercy upon me, Have mercy upon me, Most Merciful Heavenly Father. Have mercy upon me, Oh Lord, according to Your lovingkindness. According to the multitude of Your tender mercies, blot out all of my transgressions. Wash me thoroughly from any and all of my iniquities, and cleanse me from my sin. I acknowledge all of my transgressions before You, because You know everything there is to know about me. Forgive me of any secret sin. Forgive me Lord. I know You desire that I am truthful in every aspect of my life. In my hidden crevices of my heart, You will help me to know wisdom. Purge me, wash me make me clean. I enter into Your gates with Thanksgiving, I enter into Your courts with Praise and I Glorify and Reverence Your Holy Name!

Heavenly Father, You Are my Master, Maker, Creator of all things, Sovereign Lord, King of Kings and Lord of Lords, You Are Alpha and Omega, Majesty! Restore Renew me, fill me up with Your precious Holy Spirit. Let the same mind that is in Christ Jesus, live in me. I bring every thought under the subjection and obedience of Jesus Christ. By the

mercies of God, Let me not be conformed by this world: but be transformed by the renewing of my mind, that I will prove what is that good, and acceptable, and perfect, will of God.

1. I give you all Glory and Honor due Your Holy Name in advance, no matter what it looks like!

2. For eyes have not seen, nor ears heard, nor has it entered into the heart of man, all of the good things that God has in store for those that are called according to Your purpose!

3. Lord, I believe that what is impossible for man, is possible with God.

4. Lord, Do what You alone can do in my life.

5. Teach me how not to wait upon You,

6. Teach me how not to lean to my own understanding, in all my ways that if I acknowledge You, You will direct my paths.

7. Lord, I am putting all of my trust in You!

I am chosen, a royal priesthood, a holy nation, I am God's own possession set apart for Your Holy purpose. I am peculiar, proclaiming the virtues of God who has called me out of darkness and brought me into this marvelous light.

By the authority that God has invested in me since the foundation of time, I soak and saturate my prayers in the precious Blood of Jesus Christ. I decree and declare divine immunity according to Psalm 91: "I dwell in the secret place of the most High and abide under the shadow of the Almighty. Lord You are my refuge and my fortress: my God; in You I will trust."

I know that every good and perfect gift that comes down from the Father of lights is already mine in Jesus Name. Let the meditation of my heart and the words of my mouth be acceptable in Your sight, Oh Lord my God, Nothing and No one compares to You. You are my strength, You are all of my sustenance, You The Only True and Living God, You Are my Redeemer. In Jesus Name. Amen

Day 7

"The Lord God is my strength, and He will make my feet like hinds' feet, and he will make me to walk upon mine high places. To the chief singer on my stringed instruments."

--- Habakkuk 3:19

Beloved, I believe that God is the sustenance of your joy. Therefore, God is your strength, and in due time He will make your feet like hinds feet and allow you to walk in high places that He has ordained and purposed for your life. What is so wonderful about God is that He owns all time, God isn't asking for anyone's permission to do what He has ordained for your life. It may seem difficult but try looking for the lord in your situation as you are going through. Ask God to reveal Himself to you. None of your esthetics or your outward appearance matters. It doesn't matter if you do not have the finest wardrobe or the right words to say. You are enough, just like you are with nothing taken away or added. God will put the right words in your mouth as He did for Moses. It doesn't even matter if you come from the right background, have the right training, the right education or letters behind your name, or even the right pedigree. God isn't even asking your permission, because oftentimes, we do not believe we are prepared for the blessings God has in store for us. The enemy will send minions to tell you that you are not worthy, prepared or relevant. Ignore all of those people and concentrate on your audience of one, God. In most cases, most men who believed they are wise are confounded about your present state right now, because they underestimated the stamina the Holy Ghost placed in you. God is making a way for you in desert places. God is making your crooked paths straight. God isn't pressuring you to move at man's pace. God is teaching you slowly and assuredly as a result of all your life experiences. All you need is God's favor, God is touching the hearts of men. Therefore, God will make a way for you. You don't have to compete, push, manipulate, pretend, puff yourself up or put on fancy clothes to fit the perfect design God has for you. You have been taught and learned all the foundational skills that you will ever need to do what God has called you to do. David was taught in his obscurity through the tending and care of the sheep how to rule as king. David was a man after God's own heart because he did not complain in his small beginnings. David passed the test of servanthood. Just like David, God has been preparing you for your journey all along in obscurity. Where you fit will reflect the design God has been purposing for you. "Then the host who invited both of you will come and tell you, 'Give this man your seat.' And in humiliation, you will have to take the last place. But when you are invited, go and sit in the last place, so that your host will come and tell you, 'Friend, move up to a better place.' Then you will be honored in front of everyone at the table with you. For everyone who exalts himself will be humbled, and the one who humbles himself will be exalted." (Luke 10:9-11) In other words, "A man's gift opens doors for him, and brings him before great men." (Proverbs 18:16) Promotion does not come from the east or the west but from above. God did not ask anyone's permission when He selected you. Whatever God has put in you is evident to all, whatever persecution you have endured for the sake of God has not gone unnoticed by the Kingdom of God. The Kingdom of God does not consist of the just the church you attend, either physically or online. The Kingdom of God does not just inhabit your region, your territory. God is global and so is the Kingdom of God. That thing, whatever you went through was not done in a corner, but met everyone's intended ears who is in tune to the voice of God's beckoning, directly from the Throne Room in the Kingdom of God. God recognized you, you are His and He has already touched the hearts of those who will favor you.

Beloved, what God has specifically designed for Your life does not fit everyone else. What God has for You is for you and has been designed for you alone. What God has for you, is only for you and no man can thwart it, no matter how hard they try or have tried. God is the only one who makes impossibilities possible. Beloved as I have stated previously, "because a great door for effective work has opened to you, there will be many adversaries that will oppose you." (scripture reference, 1 Corinthians 16:9) What I love about God is that He can and will do whatsoever He so pleases without asking for anyone's permission or opinion to do so. God is a God who works marvelous, magnificent divine miracles and wonders to confound those who believe that they are wise, and He alone can take you from obscurity and usher you to the front of the line at any given moment, for His Glory, for His Honor and For His Namesake.

Beloved, again, it really doesn't matter if you even feel as though you are prepared or not, you may feel inept or incapable of fulfilling the call God has ordained for your life. While most people are looking for an opportunity to be taken before great men, focus alone on your character, having integrity and making yourself available to an audience of One, The Only True and Living God Alone.

God will make room for you, God will make your feet as hinds feet.

Day 7

PRAYER

Heavenly Father, I come boldly before the Throne of Grace, knowing that You are faithful and just to forgive me of my sin and cleanse me from all unrighteousness. I ask You to forgive me of any sin that I may have committed by thought, word, or deed against Your divine Majesty. Have Mercy upon me, Have mercy upon me, Most Merciful Heavenly Father. Have mercy upon me, Oh Lord, according to Your lovingkindness. According to the multitude of Your tender mercies, blot out all of my transgressions. Wash me thoroughly from any and all of my iniquities, and cleanse me from my sin. I acknowledge all of my transgressions before You, because You know everything there is to know about me. Forgive me of any secret sin. Forgive me Lord. I know You desire that I am truthful in every aspect of my life. In my hidden crevices of my heart, You will help me to know wisdom. Purge me, wash me make me clean. I enter into Your gates with Thanksgiving, I enter into Your courts with Praise and I Glorify and Reverence Your Holy Name!

Heavenly Father, You Are my Master, Maker, Creator of all things, Sovereign Lord, King of Kings and Lord of Lords, You Are Alpha and Omega, Majesty! Restore Renew me, fill me up with Your precious Holy Spirit. Let the same mind that is in Christ Jesus, live in me. I bring every thought under the subjection and obedience of Jesus Christ. By the

mercies of God, Let me not be conformed by this world: but be transformed by the renewing of my mind, that I will prove what is that good, and acceptable, and perfect, will of God.

1. Lord, Thank You for redeeming me and delivering me.

2. Lord, make my feet as hinds feet, to tread in high places, for Your Glory, for Your honor and for Your namesake.

3. Lord, Gird me up with Your persevering strength.

4. Lord, I cannot do anything without You.

5. Lord, I can do all things in Christ Jesus, if You strengthen me.

6. Lord, bring me into daily communion and commitment in You.

7. Lord, keep Your words in my heart and mouth so that I will not sin against You.

8. Lord, let the words of my mouth and the meditation of my heart be acceptable to You.

Day 7

I am chosen, a royal priesthood, a holy nation, I am God's own possession set apart for Your Holy purpose. I am peculiar, proclaiming the virtues of God who has called me out of darkness and brought me into this marvelous light.

By the authority that God has invested in me since the foundation of time, I soak and saturate my prayers in the precious Blood of Jesus Christ. I decree and declare divine immunity according to Psalm 91: "I dwell in the secret place of the most High and abide under the shadow of the Almighty. Lord You are my refuge and my fortress: my God; in You I will trust."

I know that every good and perfect gift that comes down from the Father of lights is already mine in Jesus Name. Let the meditation of my heart and the words of my mouth be acceptable in Your sight, Oh Lord my God, Nothing and No one compares to You. You are my strength, You are all of my sustenance, You The Only True and Living God, You Are my Redeemer. In Jesus Name. Amen!

Day 8

**"He delivered me from my strong enemy, and
from them that hated me,
for they were too mighty for me."
(Psalm 18:17)**

"When the enemy shall come in like a flood, the Spirit of the Lord shall lift up a standard against Him." (partial Isaiah 59:19(b)). God sits high and looks low! Man's opinions, opposition means absolutely nothing to God. You will learn "to trust in The Lord with all of my heart and lean not to my own understanding…". God is your Savior and Redeemer. God was my guide through the Holy Spirit, and He will be your guide. God will also be your ever present help in time of trouble, as He was for me, because He is not a respecter of persons. What your adversary does not realize is that, you are a child of the Most High God. Whatever the enemy means for evil, God will turn around for your good. "The Lord is a man of war; the Lord is His Name." (Exodus 15:3); God reassured me during that time that I was supposed to trust in Him. Frankly, trusting God was all

I could do, and that's all I needed to do and that's all you will need to do. God reassured me that "the battle was not mine, but it belongs to Him." God was ordering my steps, even though I did not know. It's so important to talk to God in prayer and wait for Him to give you instructions along the way. For "The Lord shall fight for you, and ye shall hold your peace." (Exodus 14:14). "Ye shall not fear them: for The Lord your God He shall fight for you." (Deuteronomy 3:22) What your adversary does not realize whether it is flesh, spirit is that God is with you. Sadly they do not have any fear of The Lord, otherwise they would not obstruct you. God Says, "See now that I, even I, am He, and there is no God with me: I kill, and I make alive; I wound, and I heal: neither is there any that can deliver out of my hand." (Deuteronomy 32:39). You are not asking for any enemies harm, you are simply following His instructions and God's will, will be done. The reason is to make manifest the Power of the Living God over your life as His servant. "So shall they fear the name of the Lord from the west, and His glory from the rising of the sun. (Isaiah 59:19(a))

Sometimes, in the midst of our weariness we can forget that there is a spiritual battle that is going on in the heavenlies of "good" and "evil," and since the devil cannot attack God it attacks the next best thing, His children. I hear the Spirit of The Lord say, "He knows the plans that He has for you, plans that are good and not evil, because He wants to give you a future and a hope, an expected end." (Paraphrased, Jeremiah 29:11) ------Hallelujah!

Day 8

Beloved, what God has for you is for you! God can move all your opposition out of the way by the swift wave of His hand. God has a strategic plan already in place regarding the adversary of your life. Little by little God will drive them out before you, until you have increased enough to take possession of the promises and are able to operate in the predestined charge He has for your life. God's Plan is The Plan. God will never leave you, nor will He ever forsake you. God will put your adversary to shame and make an open spectacle of them. God will make other nations a ransom for your sake. God has never failed. God allowed the enemy to buffet you, in order to develop and build you up in the level of your faith and strengthen you through resistance for His desired purpose. It was all a set-up. God would never hurt you. God Himself will usher the enemy out of the way swiftly and suddenly as so He will choose. No weapon formed against you will prosper. I love what Isaiah says about our enemies, "And I will feed them that oppress thee with their own flesh; and they shall be drunken with their own blood, as with sweet wine: and all flesh shall know that I the Lord am thy Savior and thy Redeemer, the mighty One of Jacob." (Isaiah 49:26)

Hold nothing to the charge of your enemies, they are not your problem. Whatever quarrel they have with you, they have with God. Keep yourself safe and secure under God's divine immunity in the secret place of The Most High and continue to abide under the shadow of the Almighty.

God will deliver you from every enemy of your life, ---"...they will come at you one way and flee before you seven ways." God loves you beloved with an everlasting love.

PRAYER

Heavenly Father, I come boldly before the Throne of Grace, knowing that You are faithful and just to forgive me of my sin and cleanse me from all unrighteousness. I ask You to forgive me of any sin that I may have committed by thought, word, or deed against Your divine Majesty. Have Mercy upon me, Have mercy upon me, Most Merciful Heavenly Father. Have mercy upon me, Oh Lord, according to Your lovingkindness. According to the multitude of Your tender mercies, blot out all of my transgressions. Wash me thoroughly from any and all of my iniquities, and cleanse me from my sin. I acknowledge all of my transgressions before You, because You know everything there is to know about me. Forgive me of any secret sin. Forgive me Lord. I know You desire that I am truthful in every aspect of my life. In my hidden crevices of my heart, You will help me to know wisdom. Purge me, wash me make me clean. I enter into Your gates with Thanksgiving, I enter into Your courts with Praise and I Glorify and Reverence Your Holy Name!

Heavenly Father, You Are my Master, Maker, Creator of all things, Sovereign Lord, King of Kings and Lord of Lords, You Are Alpha and Omega, Majesty! Restore Renew me, fill

Day 8

me up with Your precious Holy Spirit. Let the same mind that is in Christ Jesus, live in me. I bring every thought under the subjection and obedience of Jesus Christ. By the mercies of God, Let me not be conformed by this world: but be transformed by the renewing of my mind, that I will prove what is that good, and acceptable, and perfect, will of God.

1. Lord, I know that if I keep my mind stayed on You, that You will keep me in perfect peace.

2. Lord, I am so grateful that every promise that You have made to me throughout The Bible, You will do it.

3. Lord, I am thankful that Your word cannot return void but must accomplish and fulfil every task that it was sent to do.

4. Lord, I am thankful for Your faithfulness.

5. Lord, You are not a man that You would lie to me, nor are You the Son of man that You should repent.

6. Lord, there is nothing too hard for You,

7. Lord, I know that You will protect me from all hurt, harm and danger.

8. Lord, I know that You will never leave me nor will You forsake me.

9. Lord, I know that when the enemy comes in like a flood, whatever enemy that may be that You will lift up a standard against it.

10. Lord, I know that You will fight the enemy that comes against my peace of mind, my emotions, my health, my finances, my family, my mother, my father, my sibblings, my husband and my children that You will fight for me.

11. Lord, I know that You will fight for me.

12. Lord, I trust You!

13. Lord, I know that if I cry out to You, You will hear me.

14. Lord, I will bless You at all times, and Your praises shall continually be in my mouth.

15. Lord, I am so grateful that You hear me when I cry.

16. Lord, I am so grateful that You will never leave me nor will You ever forsake me.

Day 8

17. Lord, I am so grateful that You are making a way for me even when I cannot see a way.

18. Lord, I am so grateful that You delivered me out of all of my troubles.

19. Lord, I am so thankful that You delivered me from an enemy that was too hard for me.

20. Lord, I am so thankful that even though, many are the afflictions of the righteous,

21. Lord, Your word reassures me that You will deliver me out of them all.

22. Lord, I am so thankful that You are always concerned about me.

23. Lord, thank You for suppressing every enemy against my life.

24. Lord, thank You for redeeming and delivering me.

25. Lord I seek Your divine immunity according to Psalm 91.

26. Lord, I am thankful that You allow me to hide in the secret place of The Most High!

27. Lord, I thank You that You strive with those who strive with me;

28. Lord, I am so thankful that You fight against those who fight against me.

29. Lord, I thank You for shielding me from every plot, plan and scheme of the enemy!

30. Lord, I thank You for protecting me form the things that I had no knowledge.

31. Lord, I bless Your Holy Name for all that You have done for me.

32. Lord, I thank You for bringing me out of darkness into the wonderful light of a personal relationship with You!

I am chosen, a royal priesthood, a holy nation, I am God's own possession set apart for Your Holy purpose. I am peculiar, proclaiming the virtues of God who has called me out of darkness and brought me into this marvelous light.

By the authority that God has invested in me since the foundation of time, I soak and saturate my prayers in the precious Blood of Jesus Christ. I decree and declare divine immunity according to Psalm 91: "I dwell in the secret place of the most High and abide under the shadow of the

Almighty. Lord You are my refuge and my fortress: my God; in You I will trust."

I know that every good and perfect gift that comes down from the Father of lights is already mine in Jesus Name. Let the meditation of my heart and the words of my mouth be acceptable in Your sight, Oh Lord my God, Nothing and No one compares to You. You are my strength, You are all of my sustenance, You The Only True and Living God, You Are my Redeemer. In Jesus Name. Amen!

Day 9

"Be joyful in hope, patient in affliction, faithful in prayer." –Romans 12:12

Blessedness, you are fearfully and wonderfully made. You are God's refined beautiful masterpiece here in the earth to display His splendor and glory. When God made us, He did not make any mistakes. Our attributes reflect the Fruit of the Spirit, as a culmination of what we become when the Holy Spirit perfects it's work within us. It may not always seem as though we are blessed but you most certainly and definitely are. Love, peace, joy, kindness, goodness, gentleness, faithfulness, self-control, long-suffering all wrapped up into one beloved Child of the Most High God. As time goes on we will continue to "be joyful in hope, patient in our affliction and faithful in prayer, our conversation with God," as the Holy Spirit helps us to reject what is evil and cling to what is good. For every good and perfect gift comes down from the Father of Light, in whom there is no shifting or turning of shadows.

Even in our humble estate we are blessed, for "Blessed are the poor in spirit: for theirs is the kingdom of heaven. Blessed are they that mourn: for they shall be comforted. Blessed are the meek: for they shall inherit the earth. Blessed are they which do hunger and thirst after righteousness: for they shall be filled. Blessed are the merciful: for they shall obtain mercy. Blessed are the pure in heart: for they shall see God. Blessed are the peacemakers: for they shall be called the children of God. Blessed are they which are persecuted for righteousness' sake: for theirs is the kingdom of heaven. Blessed are ye, when men shall revile you, and persecute you, and shall say all manner of evil against you falsely, for my sake. Rejoice, and be exceeding glad: for great is your reward in heaven: for so persecuted they the prophets which were before you." (Matthew 5:3-12) "And He lifted up His eyes on His disciples, and said, Blessed be ye poor: for yours is the kingdom of God. Blessed are ye that hunger now: for ye shall be filled. Blessed are ye that weep now: for ye shall laugh. Blessed are ye, when men shall hate you, and when they shall separate you from their company, and shall reproach you, and cast out your name as evil, for the Son of man's sake. Rejoice ye in that day, and leap for joy: for, behold, your reward is great in heaven: for in the like manner did their fathers unto the prophets." (Luke 6:20-23)

As a Child of God, we sometimes will face countless types of rejection, persecution and opposition. Sometimes opposition comes as a result of someone just identifying "Christ in you," even so, since we are still in this life we will be tempted although not of God, but every temptation that we have endured and persevered through, every persecution we have suffered for the sake of God it will be well with us. As a result of endurance, you will receive a crown of joy according to James 1:12, for "Blessed is the man that endureth temptation: for when he is tried, he shall receive the crown of life, which the Lord hath promised to them that love ."

Therefore, we don't have to be concerned about when men persecute us, we can still bless them. "For as the bird by wandering, as the swallow by flying, so the curse causeless shall not come." (Proverbs 26:2) Ultimately, who is our judge as to whether or not sin is causeless or not but God? God can even redeem our good name. Our heritage is that "No weapon formed against us can prosper and every single tongue that is turned against us will be condemned." For the Bible also reminds us in Numbers 23:8, "How can I curse what God has not cursed? How can I denounce what the Lord has not denounced." Because God is who He is "Yet the Lord your God would not listen to Balaam, and the lord your God turned the curse into a blessing for you, because the lord your God loves you." Overall, "Christ hath redeemed us from the curse of the law, being made a curse for us: for it is written, Cursed is every one that hangeth on a tree:" (Galatians 3:13) God is capable all by Himself with no aid or help from anyone to take what the enemy meant for evil and turn it around for your good, not only for you but for many. Genesis 50:20 reiterates this theme, "You intended to harm me, but God intended it for good to accomplish what is now being done, the saving of many lives."

<u>PRAYER</u>

Heavenly Father, I come boldly before the Throne of Grace, knowing that You are faithful and just to forgive me of my sin and cleanse me from all unrighteousness. I ask You to forgive me of any sin that I may have committed by thought, word, or deed against Your divine Majesty. Have Mercy upon me, Have mercy upon me, Most Merciful Heavenly Father. Have mercy upon me, Oh Lord, according to Your lovingkindness. According to the multitude of Your tender mercies, blot out all of my transgressions. Wash me thoroughly from any and all of my iniquities, and cleanse me from my sin. I acknowledge all of my transgressions before You, because You know everything there is to know about me. Forgive me of any secret sin. Forgive me Lord. I know You desire that I am truthful in every aspect of my life. In my hidden crevices of my heart, You will help me to know wisdom. Purge me, wash me make me clean. I enter into Your gates with Thanksgiving, I enter into Your courts with Praise and I Glorify and Reverence Your Holy Name!

Heavenly Father, You Are my Master, Maker, Creator of all things, Sovereign Lord, King of Kings and Lord of Lords, You Are Alpha and Omega, Majesty! Restore Renew me, fill

Day 9

me up with Your precious Holy Spirit. Let the same mind that is in Christ Jesus, live in me. I bring every thought under the subjection and obedience of Jesus Christ. By the mercies of God, Let me not be conformed by this world: but be transformed by the renewing of my mind, that I will prove what is that good, and acceptable, and perfect, will of God.

1. Heavenly Father, I am so grateful that You have helped me to remain joyful in hope!

2. In the Bible, it says that "…a is a friend at all times, but a brother [or sister] was made for adversity." Lord, send me divine and faithful brother(s) and sister(s) that will pray with me and encourage me through this circumstance, situation, trial or tribulation. Lord I ask that we will remain in "…one accord," according to Your will "in prayer."

3. Lord give me the ability that in spite of the face of opposition that I will be able to ""gained access by faith into this grace in which You will give me the ability to stand and rejoice in the hope of the glory of God."

4. Lord give me the endurance to stand even confronted with great conflict and even in the face of much persecution and suffering.

5. Lord, reveal that I am Your remnant, made for such a time as this, "For we know that the whole creation groans and suffers for the revealing of the true son(s) [daughter(s)] of God.

6. Lord help me to increase in my faith.

7. Lord help me to realize that it is not about me but You, for Your Glory, for Your Honor and for Your Namesake.

8. Lord, help me to be humble enough to realize that suffering and punishment can sometimes be as a result of "doubt and disobedience," but in spite of these things, after a little while, You will personally restore you and make you strong, firm and steadfast."

9. Lord help me to realize "…For faith is the substance of things hoped for, the evidence of things not seen."

10. Lord, help me to trust in You, even though I may not understand, see or hear all things.

11. Lord in this process, You Heavenly Father take all the glory, it doesn't belong to me, and leave me with the blessings.

Day 9

12. Lord, I know that after I have persevered, done Your will I will receive what You have promised especially for me. Lord give me the ability to count it all joy. For I know the plans that You have for me, plans that are good and not evil, to give me a future and to give me a hope, an expectant end."

13. Lord, Thank You for giving me the Patience to endure.

14. Lord Thank You for teaching me to remain steadfast, unmovable and always abounding in the work of The Lord.

15. Lord, Thank You for helping me to be Faithful in Prayer. Knowing that You will never leave me, nor will You ever forsake me.

16. Lord, Thank You that You are concerned with my emotional well-being.

17. Thank You for reminding me that Christ in me is the Hope of all Glory!

18. Thank You for reminding me that Your Holy Spirit is indwelling in me to comfort me.

19. Thank You Lord that You were patient with me even though I did not always have the perfect, eloquent words to say in order to express my thoughts into words but "In the same way the Spirit also helps our weakness; for we do not know how to pray as we should, but the Spirit Himself intercedes for us with groanings too deep for words; and he who searches the hearts knows what the mind of the Spirit is, because He intercedes for the saints according to the will of God." (Romans 8:26)

20. Thank You Lord for reminding me that, "For all things work together for good to those who love God, to those who are called according to His purpose."

21. Thank You for comforting me to remind me that "For those whom You foreknew You also predestined to become conformed to the image of Your Son, Jesus Christ, my personal Lord and Savior, that Jesus would be the firstborn among many brother(s) and [sister(s)] who are predestined. The Body of Christ, who God also called; and these whom He called, He also justified; and these whom He justified, He also glorified." (Scripture reference paraphrased, Romans 8:30)

Day 9

22. Lord, I am Thankful that You have confounded the wisdom of those who believe that they are wise. For His Glory, For His Honor and For His Namesake!

23. Lord, I am so thankful that You show Yourself mighty and strong on my behalf so many times.

24. Lord I am so grateful that since You have been for me and that You have been more than those against me.

25. Lord I am so humbled to be called "God's Elect!"

26. Lord I am so thankful that You are the one who justifies.

27. Lord I am so thankful that no one can condemn those You have justified and blessed.

28. Lord I am so thankful that nothing can separate me from Your love, not even tribulation, distress persecution, famine, nakedness, peril or even the sword.

29. Lord I am so thankful that Your strength is made perfect in weakness!

30. Lord I am so thankful that No weapon formed against me can prosper.

> 31. Lord I am so thankful that, "…despite all things, we are more than conquerors through Jesus Christ!"

I am chosen, a royal priesthood, a holy nation, I am God's own possession set apart for Your Holy purpose. I am peculiar, proclaiming the virtues of God who has called me out of darkness and brought me into this marvelous light.

By the authority that God has invested in me since the foundation of time, I soak and saturate my prayers in the precious Blood of Jesus Christ. I decree and declare divine immunity according to Psalm 91: "I dwell in the secret place of the most High and abide under the shadow of the Almighty. Lord You are my refuge and my fortress: my God; in You I will trust."

I know that every good and perfect gift that comes down from the Father of lights is already mine in Jesus Name. Let the meditation of my heart and the words of my mouth be acceptable in Your sight, Oh Lord my God, Nothing and No one compares to You. You are my strength, You are all of my sustenance, You The Only True and Living God, You Are my Redeemer. In Jesus Name. Amen!

Day 10

"You shall keep my Sabbaths and reverence my sanctuary: I am The Lord." --Leviticus 19:30

We live in an age where no one seems to have reverence for God. Shamefully many people seem to operate as though God does not exist. They linger as in melancholy on thoughts that have no basis in faith, but that simply fulfill their inward lust about life. Everything seems to center around self-centeredness, rather than self-lessness. There does not seem to be a thought of God when there is no question of His existence. Beloveds, "since what may be known about God is plain to them, because God has made it plain to them. For since the creation of the world God's invisible qualities --- His eternal power and divine nature --- have been clearly seen, being understood from what has been made so that people are without excuse." (Romans 1:19-20) If this pandemic has not taught us anything, it should have at least taught us how mandatory it is to develop our own personal relationship with God. In the process we should have a fear of The Lord in reverence of

His sovereign majesty. Our present distain of the old landmarks that shaped us, were never meant to control us, but to direct us and keep us in line toward Godly obedience.

Overall, I cannot imagine parents that are entirely self-absorbed and self-centered that they do not care for their children. If we did we would have more maladaptive children in this society, than we already do, or would be willing to admit. It's clear many children have not been provided with adequate or appropriate adjustment in order to behave properly in their environments. Many children may have a hard time making the transition from their home-life to a traditional school setting. Early Learning Child Day Care teachers and Pre-School Teachers may have witnessed how disrespectful some pre-school, pre-kindergarten school children conduct themselves in the classroom and are anxious to meet parents who reared them, but many of these parents are no-shows for parent-teacher conferences throughout the school year. Young children may outwardly display behavior that exhibits that of their parents. It is not considered abnormal for a child to speak to an adult with an extreme lack of respect or use profanity. It is apparent we can see the Bible manifesting itself in this modern age, "Father will be divided against son and son against father; mother against daughter and daughter against mother; and mother-in-law against daughter-in-law and daughter-in law against mother-in-law." (Luke 12:53) "This know also, that in the last days perilous times shall come. For men shall be lovers of their own selves, covetous, boasters, proud, blasphemers, disobedient to parents, unthankful, unholy, Without natural affection, trucebreakers, false accusers, incontinent, fierce, despisers of those that are good, Traitors, heady, high-minded, lovers of pleasures more than lovers of God;" (2 Timothy 3:1-4)

Selfishness has clearly reared it's ugly head running rampant in our society without mercy for any of us. Some of us continue in sin, believing that grace will abound, saying God is a loving God. If they read the scriptures clearly, they will certainly find that God is a loving God, but God is also a God of wrath and not to be played with.

Some people have respect for one another, and some certainly have no reverence for God. Over the years we seemed to have control over what we could do. We had no limitations. However, the pandemic was a rude awakening for us all when it hit unexpectantly in 2019, quickly spewed over into 2022. Covid 19, let us all know how very vulnerable we all really were and as a result people had to sequester themselves, sometimes alone and sometimes with family members. They found out through the sequestering that they did not even really know their family members, because we were all caught up of the hustle and bustle of our lives. Some of us found that we were living with people we did not want to know anymore.

According to the Centers for Disease Control and Prevention, as of June 2020, 13% of Americans reported starting or increasing substance use as a way of coping with stress or emotions related to Covid-19. In addition, The Life

Project, a source of global online news highlighted by the BBC exposed the rise of divorce during the pandemic. One article, "Why the pandemic is causing spikes in break-ups and divorces" by Maddy Savage (Dated December 6, 2020). Divorces are becoming increasing common worldwide. A British law firm logged a 122% increase in inquiries about divorce between July and October compared to the same period the previous year. All of the answers cannot be found in any article, but overall we can conclude that worldwide there has been an overall decay of the family unit as a whole. If God hates the divorce, then we must conclude as Christians that, "Because of the increase of wickedness, the love of most will grow cold," (Matthew 24:12) This includes a spouse who you may have loved dearly prior to becoming sequestered with them over this pandemic. Sadly many people lead double immoral lives when there is no Godly compass within them to guide them according to what is right and what is morally wrong. Most are guided by what pleases or pleasures them rather than what is right or correct. The flesh in and of itself is lawless.

What is so wonderful about God, that in order to help us He reveals through His law the truth, that we are sinful or to make it more easy to understand, we have a natural proclivity to do that which is wrong rather than to do what is right. Therefore, it is our responsibility, and it precludes us to govern ourselves, govern our bodies to do what is right rather than what is wrong. Since in our unGodly fleshly nature, we are incapable in our state of sin to do what is right, we need to lean on God and ask Him to help us so that He can change our ways and transform our minds to do what is right. Oftentimes, what we fail to realize is that love is not a feeling, but a commitment. If we continue not to be governed then what is stopping us from murdering, stealing, and conducting ourselves in other self-destructive ways?

Apostle Paul sheds some insight on our behavior, "Well then, am I suggesting that the law of God is sinful? Of course not! In fact, it was the law that showed me my sin. I would never have known that coveting is wrong if the law had not said, "You must not covet. But sin used this command to arouse all kinds of covetous desires within me! If there were no law, sin would not have that power. At one time I lived without understanding the law. But when I learned the command not to covet, for instance, the power of sin came to life, and I died. So I discovered that the law's commands, which were supposed to bring life, brought spiritual death instead. Sin took advantage of those commands and deceived me; it used the commands to kill me. But still, the law itself is holy, and its commands are holy and right and good.

But how can that be? Did the law, which is good, cause my death? Of course not! Sin used what was good to bring about my condemnation to death. So we can see how terrible sin really is. It uses God's good commands for its own evil purposes." (Romans 7:7-13)

In our flesh dwells no good thing. As a result, we will inevitably struggle with sin.

"So the trouble is not with the law, for it is spiritual and good. The trouble is with me, for I am all too human, a slave to sin. I don't really understand myself, for I want to do what is right, but I don't do it. Instead, I do what I hate. But if I know that what I am doing is wrong, this shows that I agree that the law is good. So I am not the one doing wrong; it is sin living in me that does it." (Romans 7:14-17)

Ultimately, we should not beat up on ourselves completely, we do share a responsibility to know that when we are doing wrong, we need to get sober about every situation and circumstance that we are aware of that is not right. Often times, we can be led astray by our hearts and emotions, which only God knows can be deceitful and desperately wicked. We should not be controlled by our feelings. If we do so we can blind our own hearts and minds continuing to do what is not right and lawless simply because it pleases us, then begin to justify what is not right. Our sinful nature is wicked to it's core, our sinful nature is selfish and self-centered only concerned about what is pleasing to it. It doesn't care about the repercussions that our behavior causes others. Let's delve a bit further into what Paul is telling us in the following concluding passages in Romans 7:14-25:

"And I know that nothing good lives in me, that is, in my sinful nature. I want to do what is right, but I can't. I want to do what is good, but I don't. I don't want to do what is wrong, but I do it anyway. But if I do what I don't want to do, I am not really the one doing wrong; it is sin living in me that does it."

Day 10

"I have discovered this principle of life—that when I want to do what is right, I inevitably do what is wrong. I love God's law with all my heart. But there is another power[c] within me that is at war with my mind. This power makes me a slave to the sin that is still within me."

"Oh, what a miserable person I am! Who will free me from this life that is dominated by sin and death? Thank God! The answer is in Jesus Christ our Lord. So you see how it is: In my mind I really want to obey God's law, but because of my sinful nature I am a slave to sin."

PRAYER

Heavenly Father, I come boldly before the Throne of Grace, knowing that You are faithful and just to forgive me of my sin and cleanse me from all unrighteousness. I ask You to forgive me of any sin that I may have committed by thought, word, or deed against Your divine Majesty. Have Mercy upon me, Have mercy upon me, Most Merciful Heavenly Father. Have mercy upon me, Oh Lord, according to Your lovingkindness. According to the multitude of Your tender mercies, blot out all of my transgressions. Wash me thoroughly from any and all of my iniquities, and cleanse me from my sin. I acknowledge all of my transgressions before You, because You know everything there is to know about me. Forgive me of any secret sin. Forgive me Lord.

I know You desire that I am truthful in every aspect of my life. In my hidden crevices of my heart, You will help me to know wisdom. Purge me, wash me make me clean. I enter into Your gates with Thanksgiving, I enter into Your courts with Praise and I Glorify and Reverence Your Holy Name!

Heavenly Father, You Are my Master, Maker, Creator of all things, Sovereign Lord, King of Kings and Lord of Lords, You Are Alpha and Omega, Majesty! Restore Renew me, fill me up with Your precious Holy Spirit. Let the same mind that is in Christ Jesus, live in me. I bring every thought under the subjection and obedience of Jesus Christ. By the mercies of God, Let me not be conformed by this world: but be transformed by the renewing of my mind, that I will prove what is that good, and acceptable, and perfect, will of God.

1. Lord, help me not to lose sight of reverencing You in everything that I do.

2. Lord teach me to stay in line with the perfect plan that You have laid out for my life.

3. Lord help me not to run haphazardly after the lust of my flesh.

4. Lord help me to consult You on all matters that concern my life.

5. Lord let me consider how my behavior affects other Christians who are in the faith.

6. Lord humble me to take responsibility for everything that I do.

7. Lord, I realize that Your word is a two-edged sword, while there is a lesson for others let me also take the time to consider the lesson for myself.

I am chosen, a royal priesthood, a holy nation, I am God's own possession set apart for Your Holy purpose. I am peculiar, proclaiming the virtues of God who has called me out of darkness and brought me into this marvelous light.

By the authority that God has invested in me since the foundation of time, I soak and saturate my prayers in the precious Blood of Jesus Christ. I decree and declare divine immunity according to Psalm 91: "I dwell in the secret place of the most High and abide under the shadow of the Almighty. Lord You are my refuge and my fortress: my God; in You I will trust."

I know that every good and perfect gift that comes down from the Father of lights is already mine in Jesus Name. Let the meditation of my heart and the words of my mouth be acceptable in Your sight, Oh Lord my God, Nothing and No one compares to You. You are my strength, You are all of my sustenance, You The Only True and Living God, You Are my Redeemer. In Jesus Name. Amen!

Day 11

"Shall we accept good from God, and not trouble?"

(Scripture Reverence, Job 2:10)

We operate the same way today as the Children of Israel did in the Old Testament. No matter how many miraculous events that God took them through. No matter how many times God destroyed and subdued their enemy they would revert back to mumbling and complaining as though God had not already proved His faithfulness time and time again. When we reflect on how far God has taken us, from our childhood until now we can see His hand over the entirety of our lives. We may even be able to remember that God took us through every season, through what is pitfall and triumph, through the good, the bad and the ugly. As you read Exodus Chapter 16, you will note ten times that God repeated the same thing to His people. God's ears are not too far to hear or His hands to far from saving. That is not only the message to the Children of Israel, but this is His message to you as well... "I have heard the grumbling of the Israelites. Tell them, 'At twilight you will eat meat, and in the morning you will be filled with bread. Then you will know that I am the LORD your God.'" (Exodus 16:12) Do you know that God will make other nations a ransom for your sake as a Child of God? God is closer than even your brother, sister, mother, father, immediate family member and best friend. God sticks closer than a brother, never taking You for granted or failing to grant You every promise that He has especially ordained for your life. In this section, please reflect on how good God has been to you. Sometimes at the mere thought of Jesus, I can become speechless, because He has been better to me than I could have ever been to myself.

PRAYER

Heavenly Father, I come boldly before the Throne of Grace, knowing that You are faithful and just to forgive me of my sin and cleanse me from all unrighteousness. I ask You to forgive me of any sin that I may have committed by thought, word, or deed against Your divine Majesty. Have Mercy upon me, Have mercy upon me, Most Merciful Heavenly Father. Have mercy upon me, Oh Lord, according to Your lovingkindness. According to the multitude of Your tender mercies, blot out all of my transgressions. Wash me thoroughly from any and all of my iniquities, and cleanse

Day 11

me from my sin. I acknowledge all of my transgressions before You, because You know everything there is to know about me. Forgive me of any secret sin. Forgive me Lord. I know You desire that I am truthful in every aspect of my life. In my hidden crevices of my heart, You will help me to know wisdom. Purge me, wash me make me clean. I enter into Your gates with Thanksgiving, I enter into Your courts with Praise and I Glorify and Reverence Your Holy Name!

Heavenly Father, You Are my Master, Maker, Creator of all things, Sovereign Lord, King of Kings and Lord of Lords, You Are Alpha and Omega, Majesty! Restore Renew me, fill me up with Your precious Holy Spirit. Let the same mind that is in Christ Jesus, live in me. I bring every thought under the subjection and obedience of Jesus Christ. By the mercies of God, Let me not be conformed by this world: but be transformed by the renewing of my mind, that I will prove what is that good, and acceptable, and perfect, will of God.

1. Lord I come before You not asking You for anything, but just to let You know how grateful and thankful I am that You have allowed me to know You.

I am chosen, a royal priesthood, a holy nation, I am God's own possession set apart for Your Holy purpose. I am peculiar, proclaiming the virtues of God who has called me out of darkness and brought me into this marvelous light.

By the authority that God has invested in me since the foundation of time, I soak and saturate my prayers in the precious Blood of Jesus Christ. I decree and declare divine immunity according to Psalm 91: "I dwell in the secret place of the most High and abide under the shadow of the Almighty. Lord You are my refuge and my fortress: my God; in You I will trust."

I know that every good and perfect gift that comes down from the Father of lights is already mine in Jesus Name. Let the meditation of my heart and the words of my mouth be acceptable in Your sight, Oh Lord my God, Nothing and No one compares to You. You are my strength, You are all of my sustenance, You The Only True and Living God, You Are my Redeemer. In Jesus Name. Amen!

Day 12

"The temptations in your life are no different from what others experience. And God is faithful. He will not allow the temptation to be more than you can stand. When you are tempted, He will show you a way out so that you can endure." (1 Corinthians 10:13)

The cycle always repeats itself Beloved, once God takes us through one trial, rest assured, there will always be another situation or circumstance. I have heard some saints use the term, "Another level, another devil."

Sometimes our trials are evident, we can recognize our trial clearly. Then again, trials can catch us off-guard pressing us into a state of loss suddenly like Job as though it's a whirlwind. God may even give You a forewarning or a sign in advance or You may say something that gives You an indication of what You are about to experience if you pay attention. Prior to my own personal trial, I recall telling someone that if I lost my job I would still continue to trust

God, because I believed God was my provider and not the job. I believed that God would make a way for me. I had no idea that I would face a serious situation later, then God brought that statement that I made back to my remembrance. It was painful, but I could take solace in His forewarning while in the thrust of an unpredictable situation that God was always near.

Many of us say many things but we really do not mean them. Many of us can talk a good talk, or believe that we can handle a great trial, but the truth be told, we are not prepared. Life can throw you some really hard punches and if you are not sincerely rooted and grounded in your personal relationship with God they result in devastating situations and circumstances. God tells us that we all will all be tested to some extent, some tests or trials are more severe than others, perhaps some trials may be more severe because God is trying to reveal something to you or show you who you are in Him. It is not usually until we have been put to the test where we would have to prove those things, we may haphazardly give lip service to which will define the core of who we are in Jesus Christ. It is one thing to say that you can handle a test or that "you will trust the Lord all times and His praises will be continually in your mouth," and another thing to have to walk that test out through a fiery trial experience. It's easy to say that God's praise will always be in your mouth when all is well with you, but what about a situation when things are not well with you? What happens when you lose your job, your home, when you lose a

Day 12

loved one(s). Will you still continue to trust God then? Will you be able to praise God through that experience?

Beloved, you will never know just how much you can endure, until it has been put to a test and it has been proven. God promises us through His word, that He will never leave us or forsake us. God promises through our test and while in the process of a test that He will never put more on us than we will be able to endure.

Horatio Gates Spafford (1828-1888) was a lawyer and Senior partner of a prominent large law firm. He was also a presbyterian church elder. However, he is best known for having authored the Christian Hymn, "It is Well With My Soul" (in 1873), which he wrote following a tragic family loss that claimed the lives of four of his daughters aboard the S.S. Ville du Havre, on a transatlantic voyage as well as enduring many hard trials throughout his life. He was both a prominent lawyer and a presbyterian church elder. Over the course of his life, Spafford loss substantial financial real estate investments because of the Great Fire of Chicago in 1871. Two years later, Spafford planned a trip to Europe with his family in November 1873, but he was unable to join them initially, so he sent them ahead. The steamship that his family was traveling on, the Ville du Havre was struck by another vehicle made of iron and 226 people were killed crossing the Atlantic. Amongst the deceased were all of his children at that time, Annie (age 12); Maggie (age 7); Bessie (age 4) and an 18 month old baby. Mr. Spafford's wife Anna survived the catastrophic ordeal at sea. On Spafford's journey to join his wife in Europe with the news of the death of all of his children still heavy on his heart, he wrote the Christian hymn, a testament of the position of his faith,

"It Is Well With My Soul."

When peace, like a river, attendeth my way,
When sorrows like sea billows roll;
Whatever my lot, Thou hast taught me to say,
It is well, it is well with my soul.

(Refrain:) It is well (it is well),
with my soul (with my soul),
It is well, it is well with my soul.

Though Satan should buffet, though trials should come,
Let this blest assurance control,
That Christ hath regarded my helpless estate,
And hath shed His own blood for my soul.

(Refrain)

My sin, oh the bliss of this glorious thought!
My sin, not in part but the whole,
Is nailed to His cross, and I bear it no more,
Praise the Lord, praise the Lord, O my soul!

Day 12

(Refrain)

**For me, be it Christ, be it Christ hence to live:
If Jordan above me shall roll,
No pain shall be mine, for in death as in life
Thou wilt whisper Thy peace to my soul.**

(Refrain)

**And Lord haste the day, when the faith
shall be sight,
The clouds be rolled back as a scroll;
The trump shall resound, and the Lord
shall descend,
Even so, it is well with my soul.**

(Refrain)

Mr. and Mrs. Spafford went on later to have three more children following the unforgettable family tragedy, Bertha Hedges Spafford, Grace Spafford and Horatio Goetner Spafford. Although Mr. Spafford had more children, his life continued to be plagued with many disappointments and the same life stresses we are all familiar with, but through it all, he maintained his faith, withstood every trial by the grace of God. "God's grace is sufficient for us, God's Power is made perfect in weakness." Certainly, his stance of faith, throughout all of his trials and challenges speaks volumes about his enduring and unfailing love for God no matter what he encountered. Nothing was able to separate him from his love of God. God gave Mr. Spafford peace that surpassed all understanding, even his own. Mr. Spafford's final resting place is at Mount Zion Cemetery in Jerusalem as a result of succumbing to the symptoms associated with malaria.

PRAYER

Heavenly Father, I come boldly before the Throne of Grace, knowing that You are faithful and just to forgive me of my sin and cleanse me from all unrighteousness. I ask You to forgive me of any sin that I may have committed by thought, word, or deed against Your divine Majesty. Have Mercy upon me, Have mercy upon me, Most Merciful Heavenly Father. Have mercy upon me, Oh Lord, according to Your lovingkindness. According to the multitude of Your tender mercies, blot out all of my transgressions. Wash me thoroughly from any and all of my iniquities, and cleanse me from my sin. I acknowledge all of my transgressions before You, because You know everything there is to know about me. Forgive me of any secret sin. Forgive me Lord. I know You desire that I am truthful in every aspect of my life. In my hidden crevices of my heart, You will help me to know wisdom. Purge me, wash me make me clean. I enter

Day 12

into Your gates with Thanksgiving, I enter into Your courts with Praise and I Glorify and Reverence Your Holy Name!

Heavenly Father, You Are my Master, Maker, Creator of all things, Sovereign Lord, King of Kings and Lord of Lords, You Are Alpha and Omega, Majesty! Restore Renew me, fill me up with Your precious Holy Spirit. Let the same mind that is in Christ Jesus, live in me. I bring every thought under the subjection and obedience of Jesus Christ. By the mercies of God, Let me not be conformed by this world: but be transformed by the renewing of my mind, that I will prove what is that good, and acceptable, and perfect, will of God.

1. Lord, Help me to keep my mind stayed on You, because You are able to keep me in perfect peace.

2. Lord, Help me to trust You.

3. Lord, Help me to trust You in and through every circumstance and situation.

4. For the Joy of The Lord is my strength.

5. Lord, I believe that Your Grace is sufficient for me. As Your word says Your Power is made perfect in my weakness.

6. Lord, Teach me to wait on You.

7. Lord, Help me to rely on You.

8. Lord, Teach me to depend on You.

9. Lord, Teach me how to count it all joy when I fall into various trials, KNOWING THAT THE TESTING OF MY FAITH DEVELOPS MY PATIENCE.

10. Lord, although I may be hard pressed on all sides, I can rest in knowing that You will not allow me to be overwhelmed, because You Heavenly Father will not put more on me than I can bear.

11. Lord I may even be uncertain about the situations and circumstances that I encounter just living life but I know there is always hope so I will never fall into despair.

12. Lord You are not only Faithful but You are Faith itself.

13. Lord, Help me to know that every trial developed my patience in stretching my faith to know that I can rely completely on You.

14. Lord, Teach me to trust in You with all of my heart and not to lean on my understanding. So that in all my ways I will acknowledge You and You will be able to direct my paths.

Day 12

15. Lord Your word says that "But those who wait on the Lord shall renew their strength; they shall mount up with wings like eagles."

16. Lord, Help me to be able to withstand every trial, that my faith would not fail.

17. Lord, Help me to fight the good fight of faith unwavering like a good soldier.

18. Lord, Help me to realize that You will never leave me nor will You forsake me.

19. Lord, You abound in mercy toward me.

20. Lord, I will not grow weary, nor will I lose heart.

I am chosen, a royal priesthood, a holy nation, I am God's own possession set apart for Your Holy purpose. I am peculiar, proclaiming the virtues of God who has called me out of darkness and brought me into this marvelous light.

By the authority that God has invested in me since the foundation of time, I soak and saturate my prayers in the precious Blood of Jesus Christ. I decree and declare divine immunity according to Psalm 91: "I dwell in the secret place of the most High and abide under the shadow of the Almighty. Lord You are my refuge and my fortress: my God; in You I will trust."

I know that every good and perfect gift that comes down from the Father of lights is already mine in Jesus Name. Let the meditation of my heart and the words of my mouth be acceptable in Your sight, Oh Lord my God, Nothing and No one compares to You. You are my strength, You are all of my sustenance, You The Only True and Living God, You Are my Redeemer. In Jesus Name. Amen!

Day 13

"Finally, brothers, whatever is true, whatever is honorable, whatever is just, whatever is pure, whatever is lovely, whatever is commendable, if there is any excellence, if there is anything worthy of praise, think about these things."

– Philippians 4:8

God has already given you victory over every situation, circumstance, every battle in Christ Jesus, it is already done in the spirit, it just has to manifest in the flesh. It is revelatory when God reveals to us what the enemy is attempting to do, but none of it really matters. We just have to remain steadfast and unmovable in every situation always abounding in the work of The Lord. "Therefore, since you have been raised with Christ, strive for the things above, where Christ is seated at the right hand of God. Set your minds on things above, not on earthly things. For you died, and your life is now hidden with Christ in God." (Colossians 3:1-3) The battle does not belong to you, but it belongs to God when you have a personal relationship with Jesus Christ. God is watching over you. We must continue to savor the things of God and not look at the situation that lays before us as though it can overtake us, because it cannot. Our ultimate blessing is to have a relationship with Jesus Christ.

"But whatever were gains to me I now consider loss for the sake of Christ. What is more, I consider everything a loss because of the surpassing worth of knowing Christ Jesus my Lord, for whose sake I have lost all things. I consider them garbage, that I may gain Christ and be found in him, not having a righteousness of my own that comes from the law, but that which is through faith in Christ—the righteousness that comes from God on the basis of faith. I want to know Christ—yes, to know the power of his resurrection and participation in his sufferings, becoming like him in his death, and so, somehow, attaining to the resurrection from the dead.

Not that I have already obtained all this, or have already arrived at my goal, but I press on to take hold of that for which Christ Jesus took hold of me. Brothers and sisters, I do not consider myself yet to have taken hold of it. But one thing I do: Forgetting what is behind and straining toward what is ahead, I press on toward the goal to win the prize for which God has called me heavenward in Christ Jesus." (Philippians 3:7-14)

"But our citizenship is in heaven, and we eagerly await a Savior from there, the Lord Jesus Christ," (Philippians 3:20)

Day 13

It is imperative that we maintain our focus and are not distracted. Beloved, "Now set your heart and your soul and seek the Lord your God; arise therefore, and build ye the sanctuary of the Lord God, to bring the ark of the covenant of the Lord and the holy vessels of God, into the house that is to be built to the name of the Lord." (1 Chronicles 22:19) The sanctuary that God needs you to build is not one made by hands but by spirit. Build the sanctuary in your lifestyle, let your character that you develop through the fruit of the spirit (love, peace, joy, kindness, faithfulness, goodness, gentleness, longsuffering and self-control) speak volumes of your unmovable relationship with God.

PRAYER

Heavenly Father, I come boldly before the Throne of Grace, knowing that You are faithful and just to forgive me of my sin and cleanse me from all unrighteousness. I ask You to forgive me of any sin that I may have committed by thought, word, or deed against Your divine Majesty. Have Mercy upon me, Have mercy upon me, Most Merciful Heavenly Father. Have mercy upon me, Oh Lord, according to Your lovingkindness. According to the multitude of Your tender mercies, blot out all of my transgressions. Wash me thoroughly from any and all of my iniquities, and cleanse me from my sin. I acknowledge all of my transgressions before You, because You know everything there is to know about me. Forgive me of any secret sin. Forgive me Lord. I know You desire that I am truthful in every aspect of my life. In my hidden crevices of my heart, You will help me to know wisdom. Purge me, wash me make me clean. I enter into Your gates with Thanksgiving, I enter into Your courts with Praise and I Glorify and Reverence Your Holy Name!

Heavenly Father, You Are my Master, Maker, Creator of all things, Sovereign Lord, King of Kings and Lord of Lords, You Are Alpha and Omega, Majesty! Restore Renew me, fill me up with Your precious Holy Spirit. Let the same mind that is in Christ Jesus, live in me. I bring every thought under the subjection and obedience of Jesus Christ. By the mercies of God, Let me not be conformed by this world: but be transformed by the renewing of my mind, that I will prove what is that good, and acceptable, and perfect, will of God.

1. Lord, Help me to mortify any work of the flesh operating in me.

2. Lord, draw me ever so near to you.

3. Lord, when my adversary sees me, let them see you.

4. Lord, soak and saturate me in the precious Blood of Jesus Christ.

5. Lord, let me be found worthy of Your calling and purpose over my life.

6. Lord, let my spirit be Your dwelling place.

7. Lord, make my life a living sanctuary.

8. Lord, make my life be a living sanctuary, tried and true.

I am chosen, a royal priesthood, a holy nation, I am God's own possession set apart for Your Holy purpose. I am peculiar, proclaiming the virtues of God who has called me out of darkness and brought me into this marvelous light.

By the authority that God has invested in me since the foundation of time, I soak and saturate my prayers in the precious Blood of Jesus Christ. I decree and declare divine immunity according to Psalm 91: "I dwell in the secret place of the most High and abide under the shadow of the Almighty. Lord You are my refuge and my fortress: my God; in You I will trust."

I know that every good and perfect gift that comes down from the Father of lights is already mine in Jesus Name. Let the meditation of my heart and the words of my mouth be acceptable in Your sight, Oh Lord my God, Nothing and No one compares to You. You are my strength, You are all of my sustenance, You The Only True and Living God, You Are my Redeemer. In Jesus Name. Amen!

Day 14

> "And the LORD went before them by day in a pillar of a cloud, to lead them the way; and by night in a pillar of fire, to give them light; to go by day and night: He took not away the pillar of the cloud by day, nor the pillar of fire by night, *from* before the people."
>
> --Exodus 13:21-22

God gives us the enduring strength to persevere through every single trial. God will never leave you nor forsake you. Like a pillar of a cloud by day He will be there for you; as fire throughout your night, He will sustain guide and lead you even in what you perceive as those dark times. Where God dwells there is no darkness. Darkness and those things that bring fear are nonexistent in His presence. Darkness cannot comprehend light. Get into God's presence. God is not afraid of the dark. God can see with keen unhindered vision and perfect clarity with the lights off. Darkness does not cause God to quiver in fear and if we know and believe in Him, that we are held securely in the palm of His very hands that no man is capable of plucking us out, than we should be able to rest assuredly that He will not let any harm come to us.

God is more faithful than we can ever know. God heals even the fragmented parts of our soul. I don't know about you, but I have had to face many countless trials and tribulations and assuredly no matter how difficult it seemed, God proved Himself as faithful. Many of us like to compare our trials to Jobs situation, how He lost everything and gained even more than what He lost in the end.

Ultimately, the lesson that we take away from Jobs message has very deep implications for our faith, trust and our personal relationship with God. Trials, tribulations, and sufferings are a gateway to our spiritual enrichment because these experiences unequivocally solidify our relationship with God. It is one thing to hear about someone's experience, but it is much better to have experienced it ourselves. The reward is so much greater when we have persevered through and then stand on the other side. We can trust God even more for ourselves not only through one trial and tribulation, but through every issue we may encounter afterward in our lives. Our suffering is but for a little while then afterward, as a result of our test,…

> "And the God of all grace, who called you to his eternal glory in Christ, after you have suffered a

little while, will Himself restore you and make you strong, firm and steadfast. (1 Peter 5:10)

Our God is of All Grace, He will Himself in all of His Majesty take the time to personally, restore you, make you strong, make you whole, make you firm and steadfast. As a result you will find that the enemy meant for evil, what was used to test you, that buffeting of the enemy now becomes what has strengthened you. Beloved, you will find in the end that "God's grace was sufficient for you, for His power was made perfect even in your weakness. Therefore boast so much more about your weaknesses, so that Christ's power may rest upon you." (Paraphrased Scripture reference 2 Corinthians 12:9)

That is why, for Christ's sake, I delight in weaknesses, in insults, in hardships, in persecutions, in difficulties. For when I am weak, then I am strong. (2 Corinthians 12:10)

God chastises and disciplines those who He loves in order for their development, no matter the reason why you went through the trial. Know that God who is your Alpha and Omega, who stood at your beginning and sat waiting for you to arrive at the end was always there. "No discipline seems pleasant at the time, but painful. Later on, however, it produces a harvest of righteousness and peace for those who have been trained by it. Therefore, strengthen your feeble arms and weak knees. (2 Corinthians 12:11-12)

PRAYER

Heavenly Father, I come boldly before the Throne of Grace, knowing that You are faithful and just to forgive me of my sin and cleanse me from all unrighteousness. I ask You to forgive me of any sin that I may have committed by thought, word, or deed against Your divine Majesty. Have Mercy upon me, Have mercy upon me, Most Merciful Heavenly Father. Have mercy upon me, Oh Lord, according to Your lovingkindness. According to the multitude of Your tender mercies, blot out all of my transgressions. Wash me thoroughly from any and all of my iniquities, and cleanse me from my sin. I acknowledge all of my transgressions before You, because You know everything there is to know about me. Forgive me of any secret sin. Forgive me Lord. I know You desire that I am truthful in every aspect of my life. In my hidden crevices of my heart, You will help me to know wisdom. Purge me, wash me make me clean. I enter into Your gates with Thanksgiving, I enter into Your courts with Praise and I Glorify and Reverence Your Holy Name!

Heavenly Father, You Are my Master, Maker, Creator of all things, Sovereign Lord, King of Kings and Lord of Lords, You Are Alpha and Omega, Majesty! Restore Renew me, fill me up with Your precious Holy Spirit. Let the same mind that is in Christ Jesus, live in me. I bring every thought under the subjection and obedience of Jesus Christ. By the

Day 14

mercies of God, Let me not be conformed by this world: but be transformed by the renewing of my mind, that I will prove what is that good, and acceptable, and perfect, will of God.

1. Lord, Thank You for helping me persevere through every fiery trial.

2. Lord, put Your joy in my heart which is my strength.

3. Lord hem me in behind and before.

4. Lord lay your hand upon me and give me favor in every aspect of my life.

I am chosen, a royal priesthood, a holy nation, I am God's own possession set apart for Your Holy purpose. I am peculiar, proclaiming the virtues of God who has called me out of darkness and brought me into this marvelous light.

By the authority that God has invested in me since the foundation of time, I soak and saturate my prayers in the precious Blood of Jesus Christ. I decree and declare divine immunity according to Psalm 91: "I dwell in the secret place of the most High and abide under the shadow of the Almighty. Lord You are my refuge and my fortress: my God; in You I will trust."

I know that every good and perfect gift that comes down from the Father of lights is already mine in Jesus Name. Let the meditation of my heart and the words of my mouth be acceptable in Your sight, Oh Lord my God, Nothing and No one compares to You. You are my strength, You are all of my sustenance, You The Only True and Living God, You Are my Redeemer. In Jesus Name. Amen!

Day 15

"Oh taste and see that the Lord is good: blessed is the man that trusteth in Him."

---Psalm 34:8

We are like onions. If you could peel back each layer of our soul where our will, emotions and mind exist, it would yet reveal another layer which ultimately will lead us to it's center inner-core. Our relationship with God is the same, God is perpetually removing layers of us on a ongoing basis, no one is exempt. God is working on all of us, because no one has arrived, no not even the perfect china on the shelf, no one is perfect except Jesus. We are all thankful that God is perfecting all those things that concern us. When God says in Jeremiah 29:11, "I know the plans that I have for you, plans that are good and not evil; to give you a future and a hope." God is repeatedly continuously, perpetually working His wonderous working power over every aspect of our lives to achieve our inner wholeness. This includes not only you, but your family, your children, your grandchildren that may not even be born yet. God wants you to have an expected end. When you accepted Jesus as your Lord and personal savior you automatically became a joint heir with Christ. God wants to save not only you but your entire household. God wants to begin a new thing especially in you, to show forth His Glory, to give you a legacy throughout all of your generations. God wants to give you generational blessings. God wants to give you a good name. God wants to give you a long-lasting honorable reputation. God wants to shut the mouths of all the lions roaming around in your life. God wants "every single tongue that speaks against you, to be condemned." While people say all sorts of things, sometimes not even realizing what they are saying to sound important and slay another person at their expense, it really doesn't matter what they've said, we don't know why people believe another person is expendable. But know this, God doesn't think you are expendable. God doesn't think you are a cast away. God doesn't think you're satan's bait. God doesn't give us names like "unregenerated," or "Reprobate," when we are truly His own beloveds. God is listening to the diabolical words that folk speak and God says, "Not So!" God is giving you "…every good and perfect gift that is from above, that comes down from the Father of the Heavenly lights, who does not change like shifting shadows." [scripture reference James 1:17]

God is speaking against the naysayers who have nothing to say, but boast in their own flesh. God perpetuates wholeness; while undoubtedly the enemy and it's cohorts

Day 15

challenge you and perpetuate your brokenness. Anyone who is looking in your past, has nothing to add to your future.

Although it may be hard to believe, signs and wonders really are following you wherever you go. I'm a living witness, that even in your brokenness, God does not abandon you Beloved, because He did not abandon me. As a Dear family friend told me, who happened to be a Pastor, that "God sees with the lights completely off." Then this great man went on to say, "God never subtracts from you; He only adds!" Beloved, if there is anything that is deducting from you, subtracting from you. Know that THAT IS NOT GOD. If there is anyone or anything perpetrating your brokenness, know that THAT IS NOT GOD. God knew all about your shortcomings and every single last mistake that you would ever make before you made them. God did not even let you see all of the mistakes that you made that you could have made. God was right there with You---all along, David said in The Book of Psalms, "that if I made up my bed even in hell, He is there!" God exists on all realms. Nothing is a shock to God, and despite it all, God is in love with you…**COMPLETELY TOTALLY AND ETERNALLY. YOU ARE THE RIGHTEOUSNESS OF GOD IN CHRIST JESUS! CHRIST IN YOU IS THE HOPE OF GLORY!** You will see the goodness of the Lord in the land of the living. God has brought you out of darkness into the marvelous light and He will never forsake you, nor will He ever leave you. God is a friend that sticks closer than a brother or sister; mother or father.

"Be strong and courageous. Do not be afraid or terrified because of them, for the Lord your God goes with you; He will never leave you or forsake you." (Deuteronomy 31:6) What I love about this verse is the word "forsake".... Forsake in Hebrew is called "Azab," which comes from Strongs #1051, which means "abandon(ment)," "left alone," "emotional," "discouraged," "neglected" to name a few. God does not abandon us, in our emotional turmoil. God stands with you, during every trial and tribulation in your life. What I have found is that most people believe God heals only those things that they have an affinity for, if their father or mother had a problem with alcohol, then they believe alcoholics can be delivered and set free. If their sister or brother had a drug problem; then they can believe God can deliver folk from drugs. However, God is not a respecter of persons. God heals everything, from emotional to mental problems, hormonal imbalances. It doesn't matter whether or not folk like you and they are speaking the words of another master that is not God. Believe the report of The Lord--- GOD SAID YOU ARE HEALED! God is the Great Physician! The devil and it's cohorts are such a liar. God can heal all things! God doesn't just heal your enemies and naysayers dilemmas, God heals you! God heals generational curses and when you turn your heart over to Him, He replaces them with generational blessings. If there are generations of marital failure in your family bloodline… Guess what? God can uproot all of that because He did not plant any of that anyhow. God can uproot it all! God can

Day 15

heal stumbling blocks of miseducation, no education, educational failure, high school and college even those who may have dropped out of school--- God can replace that with Technical degrees, Certifications, Associates, Bachelor's degrees, Master's degrees, PhDs etcetera. God can take you to the highest point of your career endeavors. God can and will confound those that believe that they are wise. Because God is God; There are some things that only God alone can do. God will make an open spectacle of the enemy on your behalf! According to Matthew 15:13 ---"Anything that my Heavenly Father has not planted, let it be routed out!" In Jesus' Precious Name! --- Hallelujah!

<u>PRAYER</u>

Heavenly Father, I come boldly before the Throne of Grace, knowing that You are faithful and just to forgive me of my sin and cleanse me from all unrighteousness. I ask You to forgive me of any sin that I may have committed by thought, word, or deed against Your divine Majesty. Have Mercy upon me, Have mercy upon me, Most Merciful Heavenly Father. Have mercy upon me, Oh Lord, according to Your lovingkindness. According to the multitude of Your tender mercies, blot out all of my transgressions. Wash me thoroughly from any and all of my iniquities, and cleanse me from my sin. I acknowledge all of my transgressions before You, because You know everything there is to know about me. Forgive me of any secret sin. Forgive me Lord. I know You desire that I am truthful in every aspect of my life. In my hidden crevices of my heart, You will help me to know wisdom. Purge me, wash me make me clean. I enter into Your gates with Thanksgiving, I enter into Your courts with Praise and I Glorify and Reverence Your Holy Name!

Heavenly Father, You Are my Master, Maker, Creator of all things, Sovereign Lord, King of Kings and Lord of Lords, You Are Alpha and Omega, Majesty! Restore Renew me, fill me up with Your precious Holy Spirit. Let the same mind that is in Christ Jesus, live in me. I bring every thought under the subjection and obedience of Jesus Christ. By the mercies of God, Let me not be conformed by this world: but be transformed by the renewing of my mind, that I will prove what is that good, and acceptable, and perfect, will of God.

1. Lord, Your word says that if I carefully follow all of Your commandments, then I will be blessed.

2. Lord, I have sought You and found You and know that You are good, that You are faithful, You have preserved, protected and delivered me from every siege of the enemy in my health, my finances, in my homelife, in my employment, in my prospects. In every way You have been faithful.

Day 15

3. Lord, Thank You for blessing every aspect of my life.

4. Lord, Thank You for revealing to me that I am Your remnant.

I am chosen, a royal priesthood, a holy nation, I am God's own possession set apart for Your Holy purpose. I am peculiar, proclaiming the virtues of God who has called me out of darkness and brought me into this marvelous light.

By the authority that God has invested in me since the foundation of time, I soak and saturate my prayers in the precious Blood of Jesus Christ. I decree and declare divine immunity according to Psalm 91: "I dwell in the secret place of the most High and abide under the shadow of the Almighty. Lord You are my refuge and my fortress: my God; in You I will trust."

I know that every good and perfect gift that comes down from the Father of lights is already mine in Jesus Name. Let the meditation of my heart and the words of my mouth be acceptable in Your sight, Oh Lord my God, Nothing and No one compares to You. You are my strength, You are all of my sustenance, You The Only True and Living God, You Are my Redeemer. In Jesus Name. Amen!

Day 16

> "In the six hundredth year of Noah's life, in the second month, the seventeenth day of the month, on that day all of the fountains of the great deep were broken up, and the windows of heaven were opened."
> —**Genesis 7:11**

The Flood began because of the foundations of the sea underneath the water in the deep broke open. Unbeknownst to many of us, there is a lot of activity going on undersea in our oceans. Our earth's crust is made up of at least seven plates sort of like puzzle pieces that cover a molten core. As these plates shift back and forth, they can cause energy to build up from this friction and as a result cause earthquakes as well as volcanic eruptions occur in some cases which can lead to tsunamis. Although all these occurrences are unseen, we know that something shifted in the atmosphere because the water rises above where it is visible. You could sort of explain the explosions or frictions as a form of an opening at the core or a gateway. You can also be on the verge of a spiritual cataclysmic uprising for the Glory of God!

Open heavens are being used frequently in these End Times. The Bible reminds us in the following passages that there will be a pouring out of God's spirit amongst the people,

Joel 2:28-30 says,

"And it shall come to pass afterward, that I will pour out my spirit upon all flesh; and your sons and your daughters shall prophesy, your old men shall dream dreams, your young men shall see visions: And also upon the servants and upon the handmaids in those days will I pour out my spirit. And I will shew wonders in the heavens and in the earth, blood, and fire, and pillars of smoke."

Acts 2:17-19 confirms in scripture,

'In the last days,' God says, 'I will pour out my Spirit upon all people. Your sons and daughters will prophesy. Your young men will see visions, and your old men will dream dreams. In those days I will pour out my Spirit even on my servants—men and women alike— and they will prophesy. And I will cause wonders in the heavens

above and signs on the earth below— blood and fire and clouds of smoke."

In the End Times, based upon this scripture knowledge will increase:

"But as for you, Daniel, conceal these words and seal up the scroll until the end of time. Many will go back and forth *and* search anxiously [through the scroll], and knowledge [of the purpose of God as revealed by His prophets] will [greatly] increase." (Daniel 12:4 AMP)

"But thou, O Daniel, shut up the words and seal the book, even to the time of the end. Many shall run to and fro, and knowledge shall be increased." (Daniel 12:4 KJV)

Therefore, as a result there is growing thirst in the Body of Christ for prophetic knowledge and experiences and this term is being used as a description to describe encounters that individuals have with God. Those who live under the Open Heaven have blessings and spiritual activity rampantly flowing in their lives and being manifested to the observant world through many sign and wonders.

Let's go to our first resource, which is the word of God, The Bible:

There are several examples within the Bible where there are openings between heaven and earth where these prophetic occurrences flourish. To live under an open heaven is to have an open gateway where God is observing His saints here throughout the earth. The evidence of God's hand on their lives is through manifested signs and wonders. We do not know the answer why this Open Heaven occurrence is happening frequently, but perhaps it is because God is just watching those whose hearts are fully committed to Him. God is the one who knows whose fully committed to Him.

"The eyes of the LORD search the whole earth in order to strengthen those whose hearts are fully committed to Him." (2 Chronicles 16:9(a)

There are several passages throughout scripture, where we find examples in the Bible of what we might classify as an Open Heaven. An Open Heaven in Isaiah 64:1-2 is a petition or a crying out to God for Him to come down and make Himself manifest…

"If only you would rend the heavens and come down, so that mountains would quake at Your presence, as fire kindles the brushwood and causes the water to boil, to make Your name known to Your enemies, so that the nations will tremble at Your presence!"

Day 16

"Oh, that you would rend the heavens and come down, that the mountains would tremble before you!"

The Book of Ezekiel, Chapter 1 opens with the Prophet describing what we call today an Open Heaven,

Ezekiel 1:1,

"Now it came to pass in the thirtieth year, in the fourth month, on the fifth day of the month, as I was among the captives by the River Chebar, that the heavens were opened and I saw visions of God."

Another clear description of an Open Heaven is the Baptism of Jesus Christ by John The Baptist in Matthew 3:16-17,

"When He had been baptized, Jesus came up immediately from the water; and behold, the heavens were opened to Him, and He saw the Spirit of God descending like a dove and alighting upon Him. And suddenly a voice came from heaven, saying, "this is My beloved Son, in whom I am well pleased."

Further in scripture we witness Jesus Christ as He makes a promise to Nathanael in John 1:51,

> "And He said to him, "Most assuredly, I say to you, hereafter you shall see heaven open, and the angels of God ascending and descending upon the Son of Man.""

We witness the martyrdom of Stephen who was condemned for committing blasphemy following a dispute in Acts 7:54-60,

> "When they heard these things they were cut to the heart, and they gnashed at him with their teeth. But he, being full of the Holy Spirit, gazed into heaven and saw the glory of God, and Jesus standing at the right hand of God, and said, "Look! I see the heavens opened and the Son of Man standing at the right hand of God!" Then they cried out with a loud voice, stopped their ears, and ran at him with one accord; and they cast him out of the city and stoned him. And the witnesses laid down their clothes at the feet of a young man named Saul. And they stoned Stephen as he was calling on God and saying, "Lord Jesus, receive my spirit." Then he knelt down and cried out with a loud voice, "Lord do not charge them with this sin." And when he had said this, he fell asleep."

Day 16

Jacob's Dream at Bethel: Jacob's Ladder describes an Open Heaven--

Genesis 28:10-17

Meanwhile, Jacob left Beersheba and traveled toward Haran. At sundown he arrived at a good place to set up camp and stopped there for the night. Jacob found a stone to rest his head against and lay down to sleep. As he slept, he dreamed of a stairway that reached from the earth up to heaven. And he saw the angels of God going up and down the stairway.

At the top of the stairway stood the Lord, and he said, "I am the Lord, the God of your grandfather Abraham, and the God of your father, Isaac. The ground you are lying on belongs to you. I am giving it to you and your descendants. Your descendants will be as numerous as the dust of the earth! They will spread out in all directions—to the west and the east, to the north and the south. And all the families of the earth will be blessed through you and your descendants. What's more, I am with you, and I will protect you wherever you go. One day I will bring you back to this land. I will not leave you until I have finished giving you everything I have promised you."

Then Jacob awoke from his sleep and said, "Surely the Lord is in this place, and I wasn't even aware of it!" But he was also afraid and said, "What an awesome place this is!

It is none other than the house of God, the very gateway to heaven!"

Worship in Heaven: John's Vision describes an Open Heaven---

The Book of Revelation, Chapter 4

Then as I looked, I saw a door standing open in heaven, and the same voice I had heard before spoke to me like a trumpet blast. The voice said, "Come up here, and I will show you what must happen after this." And instantly I was in the Spirit, and I saw a throne in heaven and someone sitting on it. The one sitting on the throne was as brilliant as gemstones—like jasper and carnelian. And the glow of an emerald circled his throne like a rainbow. Twenty-four thrones surrounded him, and twenty-four elders sat on them. They were all clothed in white and had gold crowns on their heads. From the throne came flashes of lightning and the rumble of thunder. And in front of the throne were seven torches with burning flames. This is the sevenfold Spirit of God. In front of the throne was a shiny sea of glass, sparkling like crystal.

In the center and around the throne were four living beings, each covered with eyes, front and back. The first of these living beings was like a lion; the second was like an ox; the third had a human face; and the fourth was like an eagle in flight. Each of these living beings had six wings, and their wings were covered all over with eyes, inside and out. Day after day and night after night they keep on saying,

> "Holy, holy, holy is the Lord God, the Almighty—
> the one who always was, who is, and who is
> still to come."

Whenever the living beings give glory and honor and thanks to the one sitting on the throne (the one who lives forever and ever), the twenty-four elders fall down and worship the one sitting on the throne (the one who lives forever and ever). And they lay their crowns before the throne and say,

> "You are worthy, O Lord our God, to receive glory
> and honor and power. For you created all things,
> and they exist because you created what you pleased."

Based upon the aforementioned scriptures, we can conclude, from these examples the Bible gives as an Open Heaven, is a portal or gateway between heaven and earth; a place where one may hear the voice of God; where God observes His saints that He takes note of what is going on in their lives; where angels ascend and descend from heaven to earth. It is no wonder Christians are zealous to witness an Open Heaven and those who live under them.

PRAYER

Heavenly Father, I come boldly before the Throne of Grace, knowing that You are faithful and just to forgive me of my sin and cleanse me from all unrighteousness. I ask You to forgive me of any sin that I may have committed by thought, word, or deed against Your divine Majesty. Have Mercy upon me, Have mercy upon me, Most Merciful Heavenly Father. Have mercy upon me, Oh Lord, according to Your lovingkindness. According to the multitude of Your tender mercies, blot out all of my transgressions. Wash me thoroughly from any and all of my iniquities, and cleanse me from my sin. I acknowledge all of my transgressions before You, because You know everything there is to know about me. Forgive me of any secret sin. Forgive me Lord. I know You desire that I am truthful in every aspect of my life. In my hidden crevices of my heart, You will help me to know wisdom. Purge me, wash me make me clean. I enter into Your gates with Thanksgiving, I enter into Your courts with Praise and I Glorify and Reverence Your Holy Name!

Heavenly Father, You Are my Master, Maker, Creator of all things, Sovereign Lord, King of Kings and Lord of Lords, You Are Alpha and Omega, Majesty! Restore Renew me, fill me up with Your precious Holy Spirit. Let the same mind that is in Christ Jesus, live in me. I bring every thought under the subjection and obedience of Jesus Christ. By the

Day 16

mercies of God, Let me not be conformed by this world: but be transformed by the renewing of my mind, that I will prove what is that good, and acceptable, and perfect, will of God.

1. Lord, Let my Praise be accepted as an Offering before You.

2. Lord I need You!

3. Lord, I ask You earnestly with all of my heart, with all of my soul and with all of my mind.

4. Lord, I humble myself before You in Spirit and in Truth.

5. Lord, I know that according to Galatians 1:10 that to gain favor with You I cannot seek to please men. Give me the strength to carry Your favor and please You.

6. Lord open Your Heavens to me, make me a vessel of Your signs and wonders.

I am chosen, a royal priesthood, a holy nation, I am God's own possession set apart for Your Holy purpose. I am peculiar, proclaiming the virtues of God who has called me out of darkness and brought me into this marvelous light.

By the authority that God has invested in me since the foundation of time, I soak and saturate my prayers in the precious Blood of Jesus Christ. I decree and declare divine immunity according to Psalm 91: "I dwell in the secret place of the most High and abide under the shadow of the Almighty. Lord You are my refuge and my fortress: my God; in You I will trust."

I know that every good and perfect gift that comes down from the Father of lights is already mine in Jesus Name. Let the meditation of my heart and the words of my mouth be acceptable in Your sight, Oh Lord my God, Nothing and No one compares to You. You are my strength, You are all of my sustenance, You The Only True and Living God, You Are my Redeemer. In Jesus Name. Amen!

Day 17

"Above all, love each other deeply, because love covers over a multitude of sins." – 1 Peter 4:8

However, do you not know that you are your sisters and brother's keeper? Your sisters and brothers are not just your kinfolk, those related to you by blood. In fact, many of us would say they trust their neighbors more than some of their kinfolk. What I mean here your sisters and brothers are not always blood relatives, but God has connected you spiritually to add to one another's lives by some means. That means those in your community are your sisters and brothers, those that you encounter every day. It's not by happenstance that the family that lives across the street from you lives there. God has put them there for a specific reason, we may not understand some or any of the reasons why until we get to heaven. Whether or not you are their "living epistle," being read by men, or they are yours. God may be giving you an opportunity to pray for those that are in your sphere of influence (neighbors, co-workers, those you come into contact with everyday), and bring a new level of faith into their situation, if they are not already considering the Great Physician, who is their Redeemer. No matter what their religious affiliation. We can pray for them and with them, keep them in our thoughts and remember what they are going through. Pray for their strength and believe for them that God will take them through. Pray for their salvation that they will develop a personal relationship with Jesus Christ and come to know God in spirit and in truth.

As I am sure you have gathered by now, after travelling with me through this 21 day devotional that I am a Christian Pentecostal in faith.. Many years ago, I worked with this woman who just happened to be catholic and at the time my sons were attending catholic parochial schools. We would meet most mornings, she started conversating with me because everyone knew I kept a small compact Bible in my cubicle on my desk. Workplaces can become fodder for cataclysmic miracles of God, because there are many individuals with different religious backgrounds, it's a place where there will be a meeting of different religions and spiritual practices, whether they be conventional or unconventional. My co-worker would stop by my cubicle almost every day and in one of our conversations she shared with me that she watched Min. Joyce Myers every morning with her husband. My co-worker told me that her husband thought television ministries were foolishness. He would use derogatory language to describe her interest in Min. Joyce Myers. After several years of my co-workers consistent

Day 17

interest, her husband did not say that to her anymore. Every morning my co-worker would stop by my cubicle and discuss Min. Joyce Myers and what she had to say during the mornings broadcast. I would try to catch Min. Joyce if I could but oftentimes I was rushing to get to work, I barely had time to sit down and absorb anything on television. I wanted to tell my co-worker so bad that Min. Myers was just another person like she and I. I wanted to tell her to focus on reading her Bible and getting to know Jesus through the word of God for herself. However, that was my viewpoint, and the path God took me on to reach Him, but He had to show me that was not everyone's experience would not be the same as mine. One day, when I got up the gumption to tell her not to focus on Min. Joyce Myers it was as though I was having a spiritual epiphany, it felt like a hand went over my mouth to caution me not to say what was on my heart. I couldn't see the hand, but I knew in my heart that I should tell her what was on my heart, so I obeyed. Even though I did not understand everything, I am thankful today that I took heed to what I believe was the prompting of the Holy Spirit.

A couple of months later, Min. Joyce Myers was in town at the Nassau Coliseum and my co-worker mentioned to me that she was probably going to attend. Since she did not suggest that we go together, we did not make plans to meet at the event. Although we were co-workers, we were not close personal friends, so I did not make any suggestions that we go together. I also was excited to learn that

Min. Joyce Myers would be in the local vicinity, I enjoyed the way she preached. Several years ago, she preached at the church that I attended, so I was also looking forward to hearing her and was anxious to hear her preach other than on television. So I contacted a friend from my hometown and she agreed to meet me at Nassau Coliseum.

The next day, I met my friend as planned, we grabbed a quick bite to eat and made our way to Nassau Coliseum. The place was packed, there were thousands upon thousands of people in Nassau Coliseum. There were barely any seats to be found on the main floor, if someone who was not used to going to Christian services such as this they would have thought all of these people were there for some famous secular singer or a concert or a sports function. My friend wanted to sit in the upper tier section of the seats, so I followed her lead. The message was the transparent, lovable Min. Joyce Myers who has always done well with touching my heart with how she was graced to convey the word of God. Min. Joyce Myers spoke from the perspective of a woman, a wife and a mother and most women are able to identify themselves in her message. The message was so profound that before the end of the session I had made up my mind that I was going to return the next day and so did my girlfriend. So we made plans to meet at the same location the following day on Saturday.

The following day, I met her again, but this time I told my friend I did not want to sit in the top rafters and would take my chances finding a seat on the main floor. This was

Day 17

where we parted company and she went to the rafters again. I went to the main floor and an usher directed me to a seat. As I got comfortable in my seat. I took a look around surveying the other attendees in the seats near me and noticed that my co-worker in the next isle sitting alone. I gasped, it may have not seemed like a surprise for most, but it was my little miracle. I stayed in my seat not wanting to impose but knew that following the session I would speak to her.

As Min. Joyce Myers closed out the morning session, it was at that moment that the lightbulb went off and I understood why that invisible spiritual hand went over my mouth. I wasn't supposed to tell my co-worker not to pay attention to Min. Joyce Myers but to focus on Jesus Christ although it may have seemed like the right thing to do. Min. Joyce Myers was not trying to take any of God's glory for herself, she immediately gave an invitation to everyone in the audience to come down to the front isle and give their lives to God accept Jesus Christ as their Lord and Personal Savior and receive the impartation of the Holy Spirit. If I had said anything to my co-worker about about just reading the Bible for herself and developing a personal relationship with Jesus Christ, she would not have understood. I would have tampered with how God was using His disciple and servant Min. Joyce Myers to draw someone into a closer personal relationship with Him.

God wants to commission each of us as His disciples. Jesus Christ commissioned His 12 disciples in Matthew

28:16-20, to spread the Good News of the Gospel of Jesus Christ and make disciples of other men.

The Great Commission

Matthew 28:16-20

Then the eleven disciples left for Galilee, going to the mountain where Jesus had told them to go. When they saw him, they worshiped him—but some of them doubted!

Jesus came and told his disciples, "I have been given all authority in heaven and on earth. Therefore, go and make disciples of all the nations,[a] baptizing them in the name of the Father and the Son and the Holy Spirit. Teach these new disciples to obey all the commands I have given you. And be sure of this: I am with you always, even to the end of the age."

God's word reminds us to study to show ourselves approved to God so that we can rightly divide the word of God, or rather be able to tell someone about God through our own words and testimony (or experiences). When we relate to others about our own personal life experiences it makes the Bible come alive for them and speak to them where they are. Ask God to use you as His disciple and begin to study the word of God for yourself. As time goes on and you learn the word of God you will be able to tell others about Jesus Christ. It's not important that you have the best words to say, only that you speak from the heart. As

Day 17

you have studied God's word for yourself, God will put His words in your mouth. God will sometimes draw someone to us and all we need tell them is "Jesus loves them." Some of us are given the opportunity to just plant the word of God in someone's lives, but that does not make our duty less important it's just the purpose that He has for the person He sends us at that time. Some plant, some water, but it's God who gives the increase.

Pray and ask God to build up your relationship with Him so that He can use you as His disciple to spread the wonderful Gospel of Jesus Christ.

PRAYER

Heavenly Father, I come boldly before the Throne of Grace, knowing that You are faithful and just to forgive me of my sin and cleanse me from all unrighteousness. I ask You to forgive me of any sin that I may have committed by thought, word, or deed against Your divine Majesty. Have Mercy upon me, Have mercy upon me, Most Merciful Heavenly Father. Have mercy upon me, Oh Lord, according to Your lovingkindness. According to the multitude of Your tender mercies, blot out all of my transgressions. Wash me thoroughly from any and all of my iniquities, and cleanse me from my sin. I acknowledge all of my transgressions before You, because You know everything there is to know about me. Forgive me of any secret sin. Forgive me Lord. I know You desire that I am truthful in every aspect of my life. In my hidden crevices of my heart, You will help me to know wisdom. Purge me, wash me make me clean. I enter into Your gates with Thanksgiving, I enter into Your courts with Praise and I Glorify and Reverence Your Holy Name!

Heavenly Father, You Are my Master, Maker, Creator of all things, Sovereign Lord, King of Kings and Lord of Lords, You Are Alpha and Omega, Majesty! Restore Renew me, fill me up with Your precious Holy Spirit. Let the same mind that is in Christ Jesus, live in me. I bring every thought under the subjection and obedience of Jesus Christ. By the mercies of God, Let me not be conformed by this world: but be transformed by the renewing of my mind, that I will prove what is that good, and acceptable, and perfect, will of God.

1. Lord, I want You to use me as You have used the disciples to share the Gospel of Jesus Christ.

2. Lord, I know it starts with me.

3. Lord, reveal to me the purpose that You have endowed for my life.

4. Lord, purify me so that I will be prepared to do Your will and have the ability to fulfill the purpose that You have ordained for my life.

Day 17

5. Lord, show me how to study Your word.

6. Lord, show me how to hide Your word, The Bible in my heart so that I will not sin against You.

7. Lord show me how to be Your disciple, an example of a new person in Jesus Christ.

8. Lord, teach me Your word, show me how to study so that You will be pleased with me. Give me the ability to remember Your word so that what I learned I will be able to remember and share with others that You send for me to witness when it is necessary.

9. Lord, teach me Your word, so that those who hear will desire to have a personal relationship with You.

10. Restore me Lord to the joy of Your salvation and make me willing to obey You in every aspect of my life.

11. Lord, Help me to be obedient to You.

12. Lord, give me the grace to teach those that do not know You.

13. Lord, Let my life so shine that men will see the good work that You have begun in me, so that they will glorify You.

14. I am chosen, a royal priesthood, a holy nation, I am God's own possession set apart for Your Holy purpose. I am peculiar, proclaiming the virtues of God who has called me out of darkness and brought me into this marvelous light.

By the authority that God has invested in me since the foundation of time, I soak and saturate my prayers in the precious Blood of Jesus Christ. I decree and declare divine immunity according to Psalm 91: "I dwell in the secret place of the most High and abide under the shadow of the Almighty. Lord You are my refuge and my fortress: my God; in You I will trust."

I know that every good and perfect gift that comes down from the Father of lights is already mine in Jesus Name. Let the meditation of my heart and the words of my mouth be acceptable in Your sight, Oh Lord my God, Nothing and No one compares to You. You are my strength, You are all of my sustenance, You The Only True and Living God, You Are my Redeemer. In Jesus Name. Amen!

Day 18

> "Then they cry unto the Lord in their trouble,
> and He bringeth them out of their distresses.
> He maketh the storm a calm,
> so that the waves thereof are still.
> Then are they glad because they be quiet;
> so He bringeth them unto their desired haven."
>
> ---Psalm 107:28-30

Beloved, storms bare different classification that gage the potential damage, some may be mild, while others moderate, then yet still some will experience cataclysmic catastrophic results. In contrast, storms can pertain the same way to the storms in our own personal lives, just as they can shift the physical environments, they can also shift our situations and circumstances for the better or for the worst. They tend to shift the environment in such a way that we will be forced to pay attention. Storms can enter our lives as the result of a sudden illness, disease, bereavement, financial hardship, emotional turbulence...

some storms may be as a result of finding ourselves in the wrong place at the wrong time and still there may be those who make decision to stay in the pathway of a storm even after they've been given a notice of warning that an area will experience significant devastating impact as the result of a storm. Know that just as the storms began, those tides, the turbulence will turn and it will subside then cease. A storm can be so turbulent going on around us yet at the center be so calm you don't even know a storm is taking place.. How we weather those storms that are inevitable in life, can be a pre-determinate factor as to the depth at which we recover.

We live in an area which is close to the Atlantic Ocean. Several years ago, following the impact of Hurricane Sandy those that lived on the coastline experienced severe damage to their properties. In some areas, entire communities were lost and completely damaged. I remember during the storm as I surveyed the damage, I was almost embarrassed to report that if it wasn't for the fact that we found a few pieces of our roof on the ground the next day, it was a miracle, you would not have known a storm hit my area looking at my block. We did not even lose our electricity. Although devastating, property and things can be replaced. We were thankful to hear that no lives were lost in our area.

It doesn't matter what turbulence is going on all around you, you can be safe and secure in the palm of the Master's hand.

The storm had hit our vicinity, yet the impact of each community was different. God graces us to sustain storms

Day 18

at our impact level. Not everyone can handle the storm at the level that it impacts you and not everyone can handle the impact for someone else.

Believe it or not, you were made to eendure your unique storm! It is true, God will not put more on you than you can bare. God is in control. After the storm, the water recedes, then goes through a natural regeneration process of self-sown seeds. God Be With You!

PRAYER

Heavenly Father, I come boldly before the Throne of Grace, knowing that You are faithful and just to forgive me of my sin and cleanse me from all unrighteousness. I ask You to forgive me of any sin that I may have committed by thought, word, or deed against Your divine Majesty. Have Mercy upon me, Have mercy upon me, Most Merciful Heavenly Father. Have mercy upon me, Oh Lord, according to Your lovingkindness. According to the multitude of Your tender mercies, blot out all of my transgressions. Wash me thoroughly from any and all of my iniquities, and cleanse me from my sin. I acknowledge all of my transgressions before You, because You know everything there is to know about me. Forgive me of any secret sin. Forgive me Lord. I know You desire that I am truthful in every aspect of my life. In my hidden crevices of my heart, You will help me to know wisdom. Purge me, wash me make me clean. I enter into Your gates with Thanksgiving, I enter into Your courts with Praise and I Glorify and Reverence Your Holy Name!

Heavenly Father, You Are my Master, Maker, Creator of all things, Sovereign Lord, King of Kings and Lord of Lords, You Are Alpha and Omega, Majesty! Restore Renew me, fill me up with Your precious Holy Spirit. Let the same mind that is in Christ Jesus, live in me. I bring every thought under the subjection and obedience of Jesus Christ. By the mercies of God, Let me not be conformed by this world: but be transformed by the renewing of my mind, that I will prove what is that good, and acceptable, and perfect, will of God.

1. Lord, Save me!

2. Lord, I know that You alone are capable of calming every storm in my life.

3. Lord, I know that You will not allow me to perish.

4. Lord I am crying out to You in my trouble because I know that You can deliver me from every distress in my life.

I am chosen, a royal priesthood, a holy nation, I am God's own possession set apart for Your Holy purpose. I am

Day 18

peculiar, proclaiming the virtues of God who has called me out of darkness and brought me into this marvelous light.

By the authority that God has invested in me since the foundation of time, I soak and saturate my prayers in the precious Blood of Jesus Christ. I decree and declare divine immunity according to Psalm 91: "I dwell in the secret place of the most High and abide under the shadow of the Almighty. Lord You are my refuge and my fortress: my God; in You I will trust."

I know that every good and perfect gift that comes down from the Father of lights is already mine in Jesus Name. Let the meditation of my heart and the words of my mouth be acceptable in Your sight, Oh Lord my God, Nothing and No one compares to You. You are my strength, You are all of my sustenance, You The Only True and Living God, You Are my Redeemer. In Jesus Name. Amen!

Day 19

"Arise, shine; for thy light is come and the glory of the Lord is risen upon thee. For, behold, the darkness shall cover the earth, and gross darkness the people: but the Lord shall arise upon thee, and His glory shall be seen upon thee. And the Gentiles shall come to thy light, and kings to the brightness of thy rising."

--Isaiah 60:1-3

God will bring you out of every dark situation and circumstance and fully restore you. However, the pre-requisite is that you have given your life to Jesus Christ and that He is your Lord and personal savior. Then you can seek divine protection according to Psalm 91. If in fact God is being ultimately challenged in your persecution, oppression, situation, circumstance and affiction then God will restore you, for His Namesake, for His Honor and for His Glory! When you are a Christian you have a target sign on your back. It is not a bullseye target sign for the sake of just having one, but as a result of the fact that there is a battle going on in the heavenlier between good and evil.. Satan and it's minions are still challenging God. Sometimes this battle can be played out and some people may get it confused based upon mixed signals and where they stand. For instance, during the civil war the Confederacy (Southern slave holding states) vs. Union (Northern region) seceded from the union as they have tried to do repeatedly today. The Confederacy believed they had a right to continue to hold human beings in captivity. Following the civil war they tried to continue in practices that mirrored slavery in order to continue to oppress black people. They enforced laws to legally maintain segregation, as well as deny black people the right to a proper education, vote, etc. just because they had the power to do so. Today, many people still hold these same distorted antiquated beliefs that because of the color of a persons skin they do not have the same rights as others. Sadly a demonstration of these racist policies should have been irradicated long ago but still rear their ugly head and are being played out in our modern day court systems revealing the deep seeded divisions that still exist in this country. Racism is still pervasive, our spiritual arch-enemy has not relented continuing to expose and skew our religious fabric to the point that people do not seem to understand that God never divided us because of the color of our skin. Our stance on the wrong side of moral issues will become illuminated before the true body of Christ then will be made manifest by spiritual intervention from the hand of God. It manifests in order to reveal that God is still in control even though we cannot see Him or physically touch Him and that He is well involved in all of our human affairs down to the most intricate detail. There are a few examples in scripture of those who suffered great persecution for the sake of God. God says that blessed are those who are persecuted for righteousness' sake. In the end if they faint not, they will be exonerated and fully restored. The Hebrews were persecuted for righteousness's sake by the Egyptians and God delivered them; Joseph was sold into slavery by his own brothers and God turned that situation around as well.

I love the passage in 1 Peter 5:9-11, "**Resist** him, **standing firm in your faith and in the knowledge that your brothers throughout the world are undergoing the same kinds of suffering**. And after you have suffered for a little while, the **God of all grace, who has called you to His eternal glory in Christ, will Himself restore you, secure you, strengthen you, and establish you.** To Him be the power forever and ever. Amen."

I like to repeat some passages, because I find aspects of them so profound...

GOD OF ALL GRACE, WHO HAS CALLED YOU TO HIS ETERNAL GLORY IN CHIST, WILL HIMSELF RESTORE YOU, SECURE YOU, AND ESTABLISH YOU.

Was I the only one who caught that? Does it not say: "GOD, HIMSELF WILL DO IT!"?????

Beloved, Your latter days will be greater than the former days. Many are the afflictions of the righteous, but God in all His mercy will deliver you out of them all.

Honestly, I would have fainted had I not believed that I would see the goodness of The Lord in the land of the living! I know many of you are going to find this hard to believe, but there are some really lost and diabolically wicked people in this world. God tells us to "Take no part in the unfruitful works of darkness, but instead expose them." (Ephesians 5:11) I use to believe that everyone really had a kind heart, would listen to reason. Now, I know that not everyone has a good heart, most people join up with people who they know just to be a part of the bandwagon even if they know that person is doing something they know is wrong. There are people that are sold out completely to other wicked people and they thrive in doing and being a part of their evil. Lord have mercy!

There are also those who are sold out to Jesus that will remain faithful to what is right. God will not allow the enemy to put you to shame. God gave us a heritage, that "... No weapon formed against you shall prosper!" While they attempted to take my life, but God! God sometimes will use obscure Christians as examples to show how powerful He is! Why? "So shall they fear the name of the Lord from the west and His glory from the rising of the sun. **When**

Day 19

the enemy shall come in like a flood, the Spirit of the Lord shall lift up a standard against him." (Isaiah 59:19). God is all powerful and all other imaginations that come to challenge God and those who are ordained and chosen by Him will prevail. God will and can deliver you! I stand today as a living witness of the goodness and faithfulness of God who can do what no man alone can do. The Most High, that He is a Redeemer, a Deliver and a Protector. God is an ever-present help in the time of trouble. God is faithful and I am thankful, grateful and humbled to know Him today for myself as my Lord and Personal Savior and to know that He who is The God of the universe, God who created all things and everything knows you and me!

Beloved, God knew at the very beginning, God knew at the inception of your trial, that situation and circumstance... God handpicked ESPECIALLY you-----to display His wonderous splendor and all the capabilities of His Glory through you!

God is in control of everything, all power is in His hand. Beloved, God is comforting us when He says, "I, the Lord, have called you for a righteous purpose, and I will take hold of your hand. I will keep you and appoint you to be a covenant for the people and a light to the nations," (Isaiah 42:6) God certainly wants to reassure us so that we would believe that we can "Turn to Me and be saved, all the ends of the earth; for I am God, and there is no other." (Isaiah 45:22) Even "Kings will be your foster fathers, and their queens your nursing mothers. They will bow to you facedown and lick the dust at your feet. Then you wll know that I am the Lord; those who hope in Me will never be put to shame." Isaiah 49:23) For "Glorious things are ascribed to you, O City of God." (Psalm 87:3) "He has rescued us from the dominion of darkness and brought us into the kingdom of His beloved Son," (Colossians 1:13) "For the Lord will rebuild Zion; He has appeared in His glory." (Psalm 102:16) **Beloved, "Arise, shine; for thy light is come and the glory of the Lord is risen upon thee. For, behold, the darkness shall cover the earth, and gross darkness the people: but the Lord shall arise upon thee, and His glory shall be seen upon thee. And the Gentiles shall come to thy light, and kings to the brightness of thy rising." (Isaiah 60:1-3)**

PRAYER

Heavenly Father, I come boldly before the Throne of Grace, knowing that You are faithful and just to forgive me of my sin and cleanse me from all unrighteousness. I ask You to forgive me of any sin that I may have committed by thought, word, or deed against Your divine Majesty. Have Mercy upon me, Have mercy upon me, Most Merciful Heavenly Father. Have mercy upon me, Oh Lord, according to Your lovingkindness. According to the multitude of Your tender mercies, blot out all of my transgressions. Wash me thoroughly from any and all of my iniquities, and cleanse

Day 19

me from my sin. I acknowledge all of my transgressions before You, because You know everything there is to know about me. Forgive me of any secret sin. Forgive me Lord. I know You desire that I am truthful in every aspect of my life. In my hidden crevices of my heart, You will help me to know wisdom. Purge me, wash me make me clean. I enter into Your gates with Thanksgiving, I enter into Your courts with Praise and I Glorify and Reverence Your Holy Name!

Heavenly Father, You Are my Master, Maker, Creator of all things, Sovereign Lord, King of Kings and Lord of Lords, You Are Alpha and Omega, Majesty! Restore Renew me, fill me up with Your precious Holy Spirit. Let the same mind that is in Christ Jesus, live in me. I bring every thought under the subjection and obedience of Jesus Christ. By the mercies of God, Let me not be conformed by this world: but be transformed by the renewing of my mind, that I will prove what is that good, and acceptable, and perfect, will of God.

1. Lord, You are my light and my salvation!

2. Lord, there is nothing too hard for You!

3. Lord, send Your angels to encamp round about me to protect me from the enemy!

4. Lord, You are my ever present help. Fight for me!

I am chosen, a royal priesthood, a holy nation, I am God's own possession set apart for Your Holy purpose. I am peculiar, proclaiming the virtues of God who has called me out of darkness and brought me into this marvelous light.

By the authority that God has invested in me since the foundation of time, I soak and saturate my prayers in the precious Blood of Jesus Christ. I decree and declare divine immunity according to Psalm 91: "I dwell in the secret place of the most High and abide under the shadow of the Almighty. Lord You are my refuge and my fortress: my God; in You I will trust."

I know that every good and perfect gift that comes down from the Father of lights is already mine in Jesus Name. Let the meditation of my heart and the words of my mouth be acceptable in Your sight, Oh Lord my God, Nothing and No one compares to You. You are my strength, You are all of my sustenance, You The Only True and Living God, You Are my Redeemer. In Jesus Name. Amen!

Day 20

**"Then my enemies will retreat on the day I cry for help.
By this I will know that God is on my side."**

---Psalm 56:9

I don't know about you, but God has brought me through many great trials and persecutions. I believe that we all gain strength from challenging experiences. It is a kin to the fact that without resistance you will not build muscle strength and without the trial you will not grow in your faith. It is almost as if, in spite of great difficulty you can feel your spirit swell up and eventually say, even with endless tears streaming down your face, that "It was good that I was afflicted." I learned through those times of great trial, "My brethren, count it all joy when ye fall into divers temptations; Knowing this, that the trying of your faith worketh patience. But let patience have her perfect work, that ye may be perfect and entire, wanting nothing." (James 1:2-4). The reward was that despite what any of us may have gone through we will no longer felt a sting, but have great joy over the fact that you prevailed and persevered in spite of the odds that may have been against you. You have learned to fully trust God. I could look back and receive it all, the good, the bad and especially the ugly with joy. Joy everlasting, Joy overflowing, knowing----

"Therefore the redeemed of the Lord shall return, and come with singing unto Zion; and everlasting joy shall be upon their head: they shall obtain gladness and joy; and sorrow and mourning shall flee away." – Isaiah 51:11

You will find that whatever the enemy seemed to throw at you, God will either make a way of escape or let you go through it. If you go through it, God will be your sustenance and somehow with Christ in you through the Holy Spirit. Just as Jesus triumphed over every situation and circumstances, so will you. I am so grateful for the mercies of God, and I am sure you share in my sentiment. We must learn for our ourselves, that God is our ever-present help it is not just for us, but in order for us to be able to go back to encourage and strengthen someone else.

Day 20

<u>PRAYER</u>

Heavenly Father, I come boldly before the Throne of Grace, knowing that You are faithful and just to forgive me of my sin and cleanse me from all unrighteousness. I ask You to forgive me of any sin that I may have committed by thought, word, or deed against Your divine Majesty. Have Mercy upon me, Have mercy upon me, Most Merciful Heavenly Father. Have mercy upon me, Oh Lord, according to Your lovingkindness. According to the multitude of Your tender mercies, blot out all of my transgressions. Wash me thoroughly from any and all of my iniquities, and cleanse me from my sin. I acknowledge all of my transgressions before You, because You know everything there is to know about me. Forgive me of any secret sin. Forgive me Lord. I know You desire that I am truthful in every aspect of my life. In my hidden crevices of my heart, You will help me to know wisdom. Purge me, wash me make me clean. I enter into Your gates with Thanksgiving, I enter into Your courts with Praise and I Glorify and Reverence Your Holy Name!

Heavenly Father, You Are my Master, Maker, Creator of all things, Sovereign Lord, King of Kings and Lord of Lords, You Are Alpha and Omega, Majesty! Restore Renew me, fill me up with Your precious Holy Spirit. Let the same mind that is in Christ Jesus, live in me. I bring every thought under the subjection and obedience of Jesus Christ. By the

mercies of God, Let me not be conformed by this world: but be transformed by the renewing of my mind, that I will prove what is that good, and acceptable, and perfect, will of God..

1. Lord, I am so thankful that I know that if you are for me than You are more than the whole world against me according to Romans 8:31, "What then shall we say in response to these things? If God is for us, who can be against us?"
2. Lord, even though the enemy may attempt to lay a siege against me one way; because of Your love for me, they will flee from me seven ways.
3. Lord, I am so grateful that You will not allow the enemy to triumph over me.
4. Lord I am so thankful for my victory in You.
5. Lord, it is in You that I live and move and have my very being.
6. Lord, I thank You because You hear my cry!
7. Lord, I give You all Honor, Glory and Praise!

I am chosen, a royal priesthood, a holy nation, I am God's own possession set apart for Your Holy purpose. I am peculiar, proclaiming the virtues of God who has called me out of darkness and brought me into this marvelous light.

By the authority that God has invested in me since the foundation of time, I soak and saturate my prayers in the precious Blood of Jesus Christ. I decree and declare divine immunity according to Psalm 91: "I dwell in the secret place of the most High and abide under the shadow of the

Day 20

Almighty. Lord You are my refuge and my fortress: my God; in You I will trust."

I know that every good and perfect gift that comes down from the Father of lights is already mine in Jesus Name. Let the meditation of my heart and the words of my mouth be acceptable in Your sight, Oh Lord my God, Nothing and No one compares to You. You are my strength, You are all of my sustenance, You The Only True and Living God, You Are my Redeemer. In Jesus Name. Amen!

Day 21

"By this I know that thou favourest me, because mine enemy doth not triumph over me."
– Isaiah 41:11

When we look over the Hall of Fame in the Bible, it is clear who they are based upon the miracles God was able to manifest in the earth through them.

Oftentimes, they did not realize the depths and value of the ministry that God invested in them. God favored them so much that He memorialized them into one of the best "Top of The List," "Bestseller," most read book in the world entire.

The Bible is a handbook and our best instructions for every course of our lives. The word "B.I.B.L.E." can also be used as an acronym: "Basic" "Instructions" "Before" "Leaving" "Earth." and that is so true. The Bible is not only geographically correct, but also historically correct.

The Bible according to archaeologist has helped them to realize the significance of The Bible proven to be accurate down to every detail.

In 1854, Henry Rawlingson discovered an inscription in Iraq that named Belshazzar as the oldest son and co-regent of King Nebonidus. In King Nebonidus' absence Belshazzar was left in charge of Babylon.

Again in 1906, a German archaeologist by the name of Hugo Winckler excavating in BoghazKoi, Turkey discovered the capital city of the Hittite empire and 10,000 clay tablets which documented their history.

King David was thought by skeptics to be a mythical character or fable because there was no physical evidence, according to them of his existence. However in 1994, a stone slab in northern Galilee was exhumed with an inscription confirming references to King David, as well as the "House of David."

In addition, critics believed that The Book of Acts of The Apostles also was not historically accurate. A historical scholar, Sir William Ramsey and archaeologist even went on a quest to prove that the Book of Acts was not accurate. After 30 years of research in the Middle East he finally concluded that Apostle Luke, The Physician who allegedly wrote the Book of Acts was also a very great historian. Ramsey found that Luke accurately mentioned 32 countries, 54 cities, 9 Mediterranean Islands and 95 people. Unable to discount the authenticity of the Book of Acts, in contrast he found it to be trustworthy, Ramsey then converted to Christianity.

Day 21

In 1947, the Dead Sea Scrolls were discovered and they contained all of the Old Testament books except for The Book of Esther. The Dead Sea Scrolls confirmed the Books that made up the Bible that we have today.

The Smithsonian Institute Department of Anthropology has offered the following official statement pertaining to the historical reliability of the Old Testament: "…the historical books of the Old Testament are as accurate historical documents as any that we have from antiquity and are in fact more accurate than many of the Egyptian, Mesopotamian, or Greek histories. These Biblical records can be and are used as are other ancient documents in archeological work."

In other words, not only does archaeology confirm that the Bible is historically accurate, but professional archaeologists actually use the Bible as a guide in their work.
[Excerpt from ampthedestinlog.com]

The Muslims use The Holy Bible as their go to historical chronology of the events which took place to document "In The Beginning…"
Just like the Hall of Famers did not know who they are, you do not know just how much God loves you.
Beloved, as you prepare to cross over into another New Year, remind yourself to press onward to your true calling in Christ Jesus, you are a new woman, you are a new man in Christ Jesus---

> "This means that anyone who belongs to Christ has become a new person. The old life is gone; a new life has begun!"
>
> ---2 Corinthians 5:17

Hallelujah! If anyone be in Christ Jesus, she/he is a new creature. You are a new creation and everything that is old is passed away.

> "Do you not know? Have you not heard? The Lord is the everlasting God, the Creator of the ends of the earth. He will not grow tired or weary, and His understanding no one can fathom."
> (Isaiah 40:28)

> "Eye has not seen, nor ear heard,
> Nor have entered into the heart of man
> The things which God has prepared for those who love Him."
>
> ---1 Corinthians 2:9 NKJV

> "Brethren [Sisters/Brothers], I count not myself to have apprehended: but this one thing I do, forgetting those things which are behind, and reaching forth unto those things which are before, I press toward the mark for the prize

Day 21

of the high calling of God in Christ Jesus."
(Philippians 3:13-14)

God Said,

"Behold, I will do a new thing; now it shall spring forth; shall ye not know it?

I will even make a way in the wilderness, and rivers in the desert." (Isaiah 43:19)

Do you not see it BELOVED, Yes God is making a way especially and most certainly just for you alone.

"For thou art a holy people unto the Lord thy God, and the Lord hath chosen thee to be a peculiar people unto Himself, above all the nations that are upon the earth." ---Deuteronomy 14:2

"But you are a chosen race, a royal priesthood, a holy nation, a people for His own possession, that you may proclaim the excellencies of Him who called you out of darkness into His marvelous light." ---1 Peter 2:9

Yes BELOVED, I do believe ALMIGHTY GOD IS REFERRING MOST CERTAINLY TO YOU!

The Final Call

For Today, is the day of your salvation!"

A Short Prayer For You

"Heavenly Father, Creator of Heaven and Earth,
You are The ONLY TRUE AND LIVING GOD,
I believe that You Are God. Make Yourself
manifest to the individual reading this passage like
never before.
Let them know that signs and wonders are
following them whereinsoever they may go!
According to Philippians 2:5, "Let this mind be in
you, which was also in Christ Jesus,"
May you sincerely commit your way unto
The Lord,
because He alone will keep that which is
committed to Him. May The Lord Bless you
and keep you.

May God's countenance rest upon you Beloved!

May The Lord cause His face to shine upon you and give you peace, peace that surpasses all understanding even your own. May God give you peace in your soul, body, mind and spirit. May you be His living epistle read by men!

Exceedingly Abundantly Beyond all that you could ever ask or think

May you accept this invitation into the Body of Jesus Christ and allow Him to transform every aspect of your life, as I now allow Him to do a new work in me, as I allow Him to make me a new creature and change every aspect of my life.

Beloved rededicate and commit your life to The Lord, for He is able to keep that which is committed to Him!"

WELCOME BELOVED INTO THE FAMILY OF JESUS CHRIST!

Beloved, if there is nothing else that you can take from reading this book and following me along on this journey.

Please take these few words, "for every knee will bow and every tongue will confess that **JESUS CHRIST IS LORD!**"

If you do not have a House of Prayer to attend. Do not hesitate to contact our site, we would love to direct you toward a Bible based ministry in your area. Seek guidance from The Lord as to which ministry you should attend for your overall spiritual growth and development. We believe God lead you as to which one you may desire attend.

May Grace & Peace, The Spirit of The Living God rest upon you and your family.

Reading The Bible In One Year Chronologically

[Excerpt from Bible Study Tools.com]

DAY 1 – Genesis 1-3
DAY 2 – Genesis 4-7
DAY 3 – Genesis 8-11
DAY 4 – Job 1-5
DAY 5 – Job 6-9
DAY 6 – Job 10-13
DAY 7 – Job 14-16
DAY 8 – Job 17-20
DAY 9 – Job 21-23
DAY 10 – Job 24-28
DAY 11 – Job 29-31
DAY 12 – Job 32-34
DAY 13 – Job 35-37
DAY 14 – Job 38-39
DAY 15 – Job 40-42
DAY 16 – Genesis 12-15

DAY 17- Genesis 16-18
DAY 18- Genesis 19-21
DAY 19- Genesis 22-24
DAY 20 – Genesis 25-26
DAY 21 – Genesis 27-29
DAY 22 – Genesis 30-31
DAY 23 – Genesis 32-34
DAY 24 – Genesis 35-37
DAY 25 – Genesis 38-40
DAY 26 – Genesis 41-42
DAY 27 – Genesis 43-45
DAY 28 – Genesis 46-47
DAY 29 – Genesis 48-50
DAY 30 – Exodus 1-3
DAY 31 – Exodus 4-6
DAY 32 – Exodus 7-9
DAY 33 – Exodus 10-12
DAY 34 – Exodus 13-15
DAY 35 – Exodus 16-18
DAY 36 – Exodus 19-21
DAY 37 – Exodus 22-24
DAY 38 – Exodus 25-27
DAY 39 – Exodus 28-29
DAY 40 – Exodus 30-32
DAY 41- Exodus 33-35
DAY 42 – Exodus 37-38
DAY 43 – Exodus 39-40
DAY 44 – Leviticus 1-4

Reading The Bible In One Year Chronologically

DAY 45 – Leviticus 5-7
DAY 46 – Leviticus 8-10
DAY 47 – Leviticus 11-13
DAY 48 – Leviticus 14-15
DAY 49 – Leviticus 16-18
DAY 50 – Leviticus 19-21
DAY 51 – Leviticus 22-23
DAY 52 – Leviticus 24-25
DAY 53 – Leviticus 26-27
DAY 54 – Numbers 1-2
DAY 55 – Numbers 3-4
DAY 56 – Numbers 5-6
DAY 57 – Numbers 7
DAY 58 – Numbers 8-10
DAY 59 – Numbers 11-13
DAY 60 – Numbers 14-15; Psalm 90
DAY 61 – Numbers 16-17
DAY 62 – Numbers 18-20
DAY 63 – Numbers 21-22
DAY 64 – Numbers 23-25
DAY 65 – Numbers 26-27
DAY 66 – Numbers 28-30
DAY 67 – Numbers 31-32
DAY 68 – Numbers 33-34
DAY 69 – Numbers 35-36
DAY 70 – Deuteronomy 1-2
DAY 71 – Deuteronomy 3-4
DAY 72 – Deuteronomy 5-7

DAY 73 – Deuteronomy 8-10
DAY 74 – Deuteronomy 11-13
DAY 75 – Deuteronomy 14-16
DAY 76 – Deuteronomy 17-20
DAY 77 – Deuteronomy 21-23
DAY 78 – Deuteronomy 24-27
DAY 79 – Deuteronomy 28-29
DAY 80 – Deuteronomy 30-31
DAY 81 – Deuteronomy 32-34; Psalm 91
DAY 82 – Joshua 1-4
DAY 83 – Joshua 5-8
DAY 84 – Joshua 9-11
DAY 85 – Joshua 12-15
DAY 86 – Joshua 16-18
DAY 87 – Joshua 19-21
DAY 88 – Joshua 22-24
DAY 89 – Judges 1-2
DAY 90 – Judges 3-5
DAY 91 – Judges 6-7
DAY 92 – Judges 8-9
DAY 93 – Judges 10-12
DAY 94 – Judges 13-15
DAY 95 – Judges 16-18
DAY 96 – Judges 19-21
DAY 97 – Ruth 1-4
DAY 98 – 1 Samuel 1-3
DAY 99 – 1 Samuel 4-8
DAY 100 – 1 Samuel 9-12

Reading The Bible In One Year Chronologically

DAY 101 – 1 Samuel 13-14
DAY 102 – 1 Samuel 15-17
DAY 103 – 1 Samuel 18-20; Psalm 11, 59
DAY 104 – 1 Samuel 21-24
DAY 105 – Psalm 7, 27, 31, 34, 52
DAY 106 – Psalm 56, 120, 140-142
DAY 107 – 1 Samuel 25-27
DAY 108 –Psalm 17, 35, 54, 63
DAY 109 –1 Samuel 28-31; Psalm 18
DAY 110 – Psalm 121, 123-125, 128-130
DAY 111 – 2 Samuel 1-4
DAY 112 – Psalm 6, 8-10, 14, 16, 19, 21
DAY 113 – 1 Chronicles 1-2
DAY 114 – Psalm 43-45, 49, 84-85, 87
DAY 115 – 1 Chronicles 3-5
DAY 116 – Psalm 73-77-78
DAY 117 --- 1 Chronicles 6
DAY 118 – Psalm 81, 88, 92-93
DAY 119 – 1 Chronicles 7-10
DAY 120 – Psalm 102-104
DAY 121 – 2 Samuel 5:1010; 1 Chronicles 11-12
DAY 122 – Psalm 133
DAY 123– Psalm 106-107
DAY 124 – 2 Samuel 5:11-25; 2 Samuel 6:1-23; 1 Chronicles 13-16
DAY 125 – Psalm 1-2, 15, 22-24, 47, 68
DAY 126 – Psalm 89,96, 100, 1010, 105, 132
DAY 127 – 2 Samuel 7; 1 Chronicles 17

DAY 128 – Psalm 25, 29, 33, 36, 39
DAY 129 – 2 Samuel 8-9; 1 Chronicles 18
DAY 130 – Psalm 50, 53, 60, 75
DAY 131 – 2 Samuel 10; 1 Chronicles 19; Psalm 20
DAY 132 – Psalm 65-67, 69-70
DAY 133 – 2 Samuel 11-12; 1 Chronicles 20
DAY 134 – Psalm 32, 51, 86, 122
DAY 135 – 2 Samuel 13-15
DAY 136– Psalm 3-4, 12-13, 28, 55
DAY 137 – 2 Samuel 16-18
DAY 138 --- Psalm 26, 40, 58, 61-62, 64
DAY 139 – 2 Samuel 19-21
DAY 140 – Psalm 5, 38, 41-42
DAY 141– 2 Samuel 22-23; Psalm 57
DAY 142 – Psalm 95, 97-99
DAY 143 – 2 Samuel 24; 1 Chronicles 21-22; Psalm 30
DAY 144 – Psalm 108-110
DAY 145 – 1 Chronicles 23-25
DAY 146 – Psalm 131, 138-139, 143-145
DAY 147– 1 Chronicles 26-29; Psalm 127
DAY 148 – Psalm 111-118
DAY 149 – 1 Kings 1-2; Psalm 37, 71, 94
DAY 150 – Psalm 119-1-88
DAY 151 – 1 Kings 3-4; 2 Chronicles 1; Psalm 72
DAY 152 – Psalm 119:89-176
DAY 153 --- Song of Solomon 108
DAY 154 – Proverbs 1-3
DAY 155 – Proverbs 4-6

DAY 156 – Proverbs 7-9
DAY 157 – Proverbs 10-12
DAY 158 – Proverbs 13-15
DAY 159– Proverbs 16-18
DAY 160 – Proverbs 19-21
DAY 161 – Proverbs 22-24
DAY 162 – 1 Kings 5-6; 2 Chronicles 2-3
DAY 163 – 1 Kings 7; 2 Chronicles 4
DAY 164 – 1 Kings 8; 2 Chronicles 5
DAY 165 – 2 Chronicles 60-7; Psalm 136
DAY 166 – Psalm 134, 146-150
DAY 167 – 1 Kings 9: 2 Chronicles 8
DAY 168 – proverbs 25-26
DAY 169 – Proverbs 27-29
DAY 170 – Ecclesiastes 1-6
DAY 171 – Ecclesiastes 7-12
DAY 172– 1 Kings 10-11; 2 Chronicles 9
DAY 173 – Proverbs 30-31
DAY 174 --- 1 Kings 12-14
DAY 175 – 2 Chronicles 10-12
DAY 176 – 1 Kings 15:1-24; 2 Chronicles 13-16
DAY 177– 1 Kings 15-25-34; 1 Kings 16:1-34; 2 Chronicles 17
DAY 178– 1 Kings 17-19
DAY 179 – 1 Kings 20-21
DAY 180– 1 Kings 22; 2 Chronicles 18
DAY 181– 2 Chronicles 19-23
DAY 182 – Obadiah; Psalm 82-83

DAY 183 – 2 Kings 1-4
DAY 184 --- 2 Kings 5-8
DAY 185– 2 Kings 9-11
DAY 186 – 2 Kings 12-13; 2 Chronicles 24
DAY 187 – 2 Kings 14; 2 Chronicles 25
DAY 188– Jonah 1-4
DAY 189– 2 Kings 15; 2 Chronicles 26
DAY 190– Isaiah 1-4
DAY 191 – Isaiah 5-8
DAY 192 – Amos 1-5
DAY 193– Amos 6-9
DAY 194– 2 Chronicles 27; Isaiah 9012
DAY 195– Micah 1-7
DAY 196– 2 chronicles 28; 2 Kings 16-17
DAY 197 – Isaiah 13-17
DAY 198 – Isaiah 18-22
DAY 199 – Isaiah 23-27
DAY 200– 2 Kings 18:108; 2 Chronicles 29-31; Psalm 48
DAY 201 – Hosea 1-7
DAY 202 – Hosea 8-14
DAY 203– Isaiah 28-30
DAY 204 – Isaiah 31-34
DAY 205--- Isaiah 35-36
DAY 206 – Isaiah 37-39; Psalm 76
DAY 207 – Isaiah 40-43
DAY 208– Isaiah 44-48
DAY 209 – 2 Kings 18:9-37; 2 Kings 19:1-37; Psalm 46, 80, 135

Reading The Bible In One Year Chronologically

DAY 210– Isaiah 49-53
DAY 211 – Isaiah 54-58
DAY 212– Isaiah 59-63
DAY 213 – Isaiah 64-66
DAY 214– 2 Kings 20-21
DAY 215 – 2 Chronicles 32-33
DAY 216 – Nahum 1-3
DAY 217 – 2 Kings 22-23; 2 Chronicles 34-35
DAY 218 – Zephaniah 1-3
DAY 219 – Jeremiah 1-3
DAY 220 --- Jeremiah 4-6
DAY 221 – Jeremiah 7-9
DAY 222 – Jeremiah 10-13
DAY 223– Jeremiah 14-17
DAY 224 – Jeremiah 18-22
DAY 225– Jeremiah 23-25
DAY 226– Jeremiah 26-29
DAY 227 – Jeremiah 30-31
DAY 228 – Jeremiah 32-34
DAY 229 – Jeremiah 35-37
DAY 230 – Jeremiah 38-40; Psalm 74, 79
DAY 231 – 2 Kings 24-25; 2 chronicles 36
DAY 232 – Habakkuk 1-3
DAY 233 – Jeremiah 41-45
DAY 234 – Jeremiah 46-48
DAY 235 – Jeremiah 49-50
DAY 236 – Jeremiah 51-52

DAY 237 – Lamentations 1; Lamentation 2; Lamentations 3:1-36
DAY 238 – Lamentations 3:37-66; Lamentations 4; Lamentations 5:1-22
DAY 239– Ezekiel 1-4
DAY 240 – Ezekiel 5-8
DAY 241 --- Ezekiel 9-12
DAY 242– Ezekiel 13-15
DAY 243 – Ezekiel 16-17
DAY 244 – Ezekiel 18-19
DAY 245– Ezekiel 20-21
DAY 246 –Ezekiel 22-23
DAY 247--- Ezekiel 24-27
DAY 248 – Ezekiel 28-31
DAY 249 – Ezekiel 32-34
DAY 250– Ezekiel 35-37
DAY 251 – Ezekiel 38-39
DAY 252– Ezekiel 40-41
DAY 253 – Ezekiel 42-43
DAY 254– Ezekiel 44-45
DAY 255– Ezekiel 46-48
DAY 256– Joel 1-3
DAY 257 – Daniel 1-3
DAY 258– Daniel 4-6
DAY 259– Daniel 7-9
DAY 260– Daniel 10-12
DAY 261 – Ezra 1-3
DAY 262 --- Ezra 4-6; Psalm 137

DAY 263 – Haggai 1-2
DAY 264 – Zechariah 1-7
DAY 265– Zechariah 8-14
DAY 266 – Esther 1-5
DAY 267–Esther 6-10
DAY 268– Ezra 7-10
DAY 269 – Nehemiah 1-5
DAY 270 – Nehemiah 6-7
DAY 271– Nehemiah 8-10
DAY 272 – Nehemiah 11-13; Psalm 126
DAY 273 – Malachi 1-4
DAY 274 – Luke1; John 1:1-14
DAY 275 – Matthew 1; Luke 2:1-38
DAY 276– Matthew 2; Luke 2:39-52
DAY 277– Matthew 3; Mark 1; Luke 3
DAY 278 – Matthew 4; Luke 4-5; John 1:15-51
DAY 279 – John 2-4
DAY 280 – Mark 2
DAY 281– John 5
DAY 282 – Matthew 12:1021; Mark 3; Luke 6
DAY 283 --- Matthew 5-7
DAY 284– Matthew 8:1-13; Luke 7
DAY 285 – Matthew 11
DAY 286– Matthew 12:22-50; Luke 11
DAY 287 – Matthew 13; Luke 8
DAY 288– Matthew 8:14-34; Mark 4-5
DAY 289 – Matthew 9-10
DAY 290 – Matthew 14; Mark 6; Luke 9:10-17

DAY 291 –John 6
DAY 292 – Matthew 15; Mark 7
DAY 293– Matthew 16; Mark 8; Luke 9:18-27
DAY 294 – Matthew 17; Mark 9; Luke 9:28-62
DAY 295– Matthew 18
DAY 296– John 7-8
DAY 297 – John 9:1-41; John 10:1-21
DAY 298– Luke 10-11; John 10:22-42
DAY 299– Luke 12-13
DAY 300– Luke 14-15
DAY 301 – Luke 16; Luke 17:1-10-
DAY 302– John 11
DAY 303– Luke 17:11-37; Luke 18-1-14
DAY 304– Matthew 19; Mark 10
DAY 305 – Matthew 20-21
DAY 306 --- Luke 18:15-43; Luke 19:1-48
DAY 307 – Mark 11; John 12
DAY 308 – Matthew 22; Mark 12
DAY 309 – Matthew 23; Luke 20-21
DAY 310 – Mark 13
DAY 311– Matthew 24
DAY 312 – Matthew 25
DAY 313 – Matthew 26; Mark 14
DAY 314 – Luke 22; John 13
DAY 315– John 14-17
DAY 316 – Matthew 27; Mark 15
DAY 317 – Luke 23; John 18-19
DAY 318 – Matthew 28; Mark 16

DAY 319– Luke 24; John 20-21
DAY 320– Acts 1-3
DAY 321 – Acts 4-6
DAY 322 – Acts 7-8
DAY 323 – Acts 9-10
DAY 324– Acts 11-12
DAY 325 – Acts 13-14
DAY 326 --- James 1-5
DAY 327 – Acts 15-16
DAY 328 – Galatians 1-3
DAY 329– Galatians 4-6
DAY 330– Acts 17; Acts 18:1-18
DAY 331 – 1 Thessalonians 1-5; 2 Thessalonians 1-3
DAY 332– Acts 18:19-28; Acts 19:1-41
DAY 333 – 1 Corinthians 1-4
DAY 334 – 1 Corinthians 5-8
DAY 335 – 1 Corinthians 9-11
DAY 336 –1 Corinthians 12-14
DAY 337– 1 Corinthians 15-16
DAY 338 – 2 Corinthains 1-4
DAY 339– 2 Corinthians 5-9
DAY 340– 2 Corinthians 10-13
DAY 341– Acts 20:1-3; Romans 1-3
DAY 342 – Romans 4-7
DAY 343 – Romans 8-10
DAY 344 – Romans 11-13
DAY 345– Romans 14-16
DAY 346 – Acts 20:4-38; Acts 21; Acts 22; Acts 23:1-35

DAY 347 --- Acts 24-26
DAY 348 – Acts 27-28
DAY 349 – Colossians 1-4; Philemon
DAY 350– Ephesians 1-6
DAY 351– Philippians 1-4
DAY 352– 1 timothy 1-6
DAY 353– Titus 1-3
DAY 354 –1 Peter 1-5
DAY 355 – Hebrews 1-6
DAY 356 –Hebrews 7-10
DAY 357 – Hebrews 11-13
DAY 358 – 2 Timothy 1-4
DAY 359 – 2 Peter 1-3; Jude
DAY 360– 1 John 1-5
DAY 361– 2 John; 3 John
DAY 362 –Revelation 1-5
DAY 363 – Revelation 6-11
DAY 364– Revelation 12-18
DAY 365– Revelation 19-22

About The Book

Due to the chaos shared on the news, the various trials and tribulations that arise in daily life, and other various negative elements, it can be difficult to maintain a positive outlook and keep moving forward. It is important to take a step back and remember a very important fact that can make the light shine on any dark day: "God loves you!" Author, Roberta Whitfield helps guide readers back to this realization in a comprehensive 21 Days of Devotion: A Daily Compilation for Meditation. Whether readers believers already or in search of forming a personal relationship with God, this new devotional offers a fresh perspective through excellent scripture resources to prayers to real life stories and more.

Author Bio

Roberta Whitfield loves and has committed her life to serving God and spreading the gospel of Jesus Christ, if but by reaching one person at a time. She is also a devoted Christian wife, mother currently pursuing a formal degree to strengthen her devotion to community, volunteerism, and counseling. May you be blessed by her first debut book for non-believers as well as believers to strengthen their personal relationship and walk with Jesus Christ through encouraging daily devotion.

CPSIA information can be obtained
at www.ICGtesting.com
Printed in the USA
BVHW041250041122
651159BV00002B/335